WHO IS THIS KID? COLLEGES WANT TO KNOW!

Writing Exercises for Winning Applications

This book is available in print or eBook form.

Written by
Joyce Slayton Mitchell

Edited by
Patricia Gray

Graphic Design by
Scott Slyter

THE CRITICAL THINKING CO.™
www.CriticalThinking.com
Phone: 800-458-4849 • Fax: 541-756-1758
1991 Sherman Ave., Suite 200 • North Bend • OR 97459
ISBN 978-1-60144-969-6

Printed in the United States of America by McNaughton & Gunn, Inc., Saline, MI (Aug. 2019)

Table of Contents

About the Author

Joyce Slayton Mitchell has served 17 years as the Director of College Advising at the Nightingale-Bamford School in New York City, plus 13 years as college counselor in both public and private schools. The past 11 years, Mitchell has served as Consultant in US College Admissions in China, South Korea, and the USA. She is the author of forty-one works of nonfiction, including: 8 First Choices, 2017, College Culture: What's My Match? The Korean Guide to American Universities (in Korean Language), The Chinese Guide to American Universities (in Mandarin), and career books published by the College Board. She writes a college advice column in the Hardwick Gazette (Vermont), and in China Daily's teen edition, 21st Century, for Mainland China's national school students. Mitchell has served on the Editorial Advisory Board for the College Board Review and on the school committee of U.S. News & World Report.

Reviews for This Book

BOSTON COLLEGE "Nobody in her profession offers more insight into selective college admissions than Joyce Slayton Mitchell. She has a facility for making the complex not so complex, and like Toto in the *Wizard of Oz*, she excels at revealing what is behind the curtain. All who read *Who Is This Kid?* will have a better understanding of what goes into the decision-making process, what admission deans look for, and how to best present your authentic self."

–Howard Singer

NORTHWESTERN *"Who Is This Kid?* helps us understand how this applicant will connect and contribute to the community where they will study. We want to enroll students who understand themselves and can tell their own stories. Ms. Mitchell's advice will help students enormously to give admission committees what they need to answer that extremely important question. Trust her."

–F. Sheppard Shanley

OXY|OCCIDENTAL "*Who Is This Kid?* is a much needed, refreshing addition to college search literature that underscores the importance of reflection and awareness. Applicants often hide behind a generic veil, much to their disadvantage. Mitchell's work encourages readers to uncover their distinct personalities and translate them compellingly in writing, making for riveting reads for admission officers."

–Vince Cuseo

UNIVERSITY OF VERMONT "Ms. Mitchell has a wealth of knowledge and offers great advice and insights into the mysterious and complex world of the college admissions process."

–Sarah (Sally) Hobart

POMONA "Joyce Slayton Mitchell is at it again, this time delivering a practical hands-on workbook to help young people find their voice in the college admissions process. If you've ever wondered how to kick-start writing your college applications, this book is for you."

–Seth Allen

COLGATE "*Who Is this kid?* is Mitchell's captivating way of having college bound students think about who they really are, and while she achieves that goal in a brilliant way, the thoughtful exercises may lead to an even more important outcome. If a student takes the book's interesting exercises seriously, that student will build a strong sense of ownership for what should become <u>their</u> college search–not a search they have someone else to do for them."

–Gary L. Ross

Introduction

Do you dream of going to college? Are you a hard-working student with top test scores? Have you heard that many high-testing students are not getting into Harvard, Pomona, or Emory? Do you know why top testers do not always get in? It's a cultural difference in the American college admissions process. UK, French, Chinese, Japanese, Korean, Canadian universities look for students who test the highest in their fields of study and on their national university admissions examinations. Many American colleges use a "holistic" admissions method, which looks for the most interesting students who ask the best questions–who know themselves–how they think and what they think and how well they know their own culture: their history, literature, their government and politics, their art, and music. They look for what the student is going to bring to the particular college culture of their specific colleges. The application for one college should not be the same as the application for another. Special talents, leadership, the arts, sports, and more count in the holistic admissions method.

American colleges also value diversity in the classroom as much as top test scores. The USA believes that students learn from each other. Therefore we want as many different countries, states in the USA, first languages, ethnic groups, and political and economic differences, as we can collect. Our colleges ask, "Who is this American or French kid? What can she bring to our college community–classroom discussion, and sports? What has he learned about himself from his choices of band and music groups, and theatre programs that are unique?

If 10% to 20% of the students in a college are international, that means the college wants a percentage of Asians (a few from each Asian country); private colleges will not fill the entering class with students from one U.S. state–no matter how many apply. They won't fill the 20% of internationals with just Canadians or Brazilians, or Chinese, or New Zealanders. Each of these groups bring different backgrounds and ways of thinking to the classroom. It's the mix, the differences, that are important.

Who is this kid? That's what the College Deans of Admissions want to know. That's why this book is written for you. It will help you think about what kind of student, friend, son, or daughter you are. It will give you exercises to write and think about and to talk about with your family and friends. You will use what you learn about yourself as you search the colleges, as you write the college applications, write the essay, take a college tour, and as you interview online or in person. Your job is to separate yourself from the hundreds of other American and international students who are applying to the same colleges and universities.

Basic Assumptions

Here is a book of thinking and writing exercises to help you understand how to stand out from all the other hardworking, strong students with special talents. *Who Is This kid? Colleges Want to Know!* is based on these basic assumptions:

1. **Test scores do not get you in.**
   Top test scores get you into many international universities. American colleges, even the most selective, look at the rigor of the high school curriculum and grades earned in these courses before they look at test scores. Test scores (TOEFL, IELTS, SATS, ACTS) are checked for your level of English and your ability to do the work at the particular college. NO SAT or TOEFL score will get you in. A perfect test score is not a perfect applicant in the USA. Duke and Northwestern turn down more than half of the perfect ACT/SAT applicants who apply. They accept the students who are strong enough to do the work with a wide range of test scores, and who will bring their particular talents, interests, and creativity to the classroom and college community. US colleges are looking for students who have a

sense of themselves, their family and school experiences, and are able to share that assessment on their applications. US colleges are looking for students who are eager to share who they are and learn from their new classmates from all over the world.

2. **Personalize the process–be authentically you.**
Remember this–the college admissions dean is looking for ways to choose one academically qualified student over another. There is not room on campus for every qualified student who applies. Your job is to give them reasons why you are the best applicant for their college–and you must do that by showing them how being you will add interesting conversation to their college classroom discussion. Your application and essay must add an understanding to the life in the dormitories, in the clubs, in the social lives of your classmates. In the exercises of this book, think about how you separate yourself from the rest of the world in what you have experienced and learned about growing up in the USA or your country, with a particular history, art, literature, food, and music that determines your culture. Think and write about growing up in your family. These are the things that will make you stand out and why the colleges look for the qualified students who know that they are who they are because they are from a particular part of the USA or a specific nation.

Acknowledgments

The primary resources for *Who Is This Kid? Colleges Want to Know!* are the voices of college-bound American and international high school students I have met, listened to, and heard through their questions in my U.S. college admissions career in public and private schools in the USA, China, and Korea.

Dedication

This book is dedicated to my grandson, René Mahardika Edward Mitchell, a pre-school boy in Coloane, Macau. It is also dedicated to the brave and courageous high school students of America and the world who all face the experience of every adult they know giving them advice about where to go to college. The international students who come to the USA for college from a land far away from their families and friends require extra courage. Americans and internationals alike, you are the hope of the world as you strive in your college and career for understanding toward a peaceful global life and economy with harmony of our cultural differences.

Joyce Slayton Mitchell
New York City, Vermont, and Shanghai

Part I
Student Self-Assessment: Thinking and Writing Exercises

Bright and Creative Ways to Think About You

Think about who you are before you write these self-assessment exercises. The colleges want to know how you describe yourself. Below is a list of adjectives and descriptive words to help you get started on your book exercises. There are no excuses for you not to be able to describe yourself, or how you think others describe you, after you study this list.

Personal Quality Words

accepting
accurate
achieving
adaptable
adventurous
alert
alive
altruistic
amazing
ambitious
analytical
appreciative
artistic
assertive
attentive
authentic
aware
balanced
blissful
blooming
bold
bountiful
brave
breath-taking
bright
calm
careful
carefree
caring
cautious
centered
certain
charitable
cheeky
cheerful
chirpy
civic-Minded

clean
colorful
competitive
clear-thinking
communicative
compassionate
compatible
competitive
complete
confident
conscientious
considerate
conservative
consistent
content
co-operative
courageous
conscientious
courteous
creative
curious
cultural
decisive
deliberate
dependable
desirable
determined
devoted
disciplined
discrete
discriminating
easy-going
eager
efficient
empathetic
energetic
enlightened

enthusiastic
entrepreneurial
experienced
fair-minded
faithful
farsighted
fast-learner
feeling
fierce
flexible
flourishing
focused
forgiving
fortuitous
free
fresh
friendly
frugal
funny
generous
good
gratuitous
great
happy
harmonious
healthy
helpful
holistic
hopeful
humble
humorous
honest
humble
idealistic
imaginative
having integrity
independent

individualistic
industrious
innovative
insightful
intelligent
intense
intuitive
inventive
joyful
just
kind
leading or
leader
learned
loving
loyal
lucky
mature
moral
motivating
natural
neat
needed
noticeable
nurturing
obedient
objective
open
optimistic
original
organized
outgoing
passionate
patient
peaceful
perceptive
persevering

persistent
persuasive
playful
poetic
polite
popular
powerful
practical
precise
profound
progressive
proud
professional
punctual
purposeful
questioning
quick-witted
realistic
refreshing
reliable
resilient
resourceful
respectful
responsible
selfless
self-aware
self-confident
self-disciplined
sensitive
serene
skilled
smart
smooth
special
spectacular
spiritual
spontaneous

stable
steadfast
strategic
strong
strong-willed
stylish
successful
supportive
supreme
sympathetic
tactful
talented
tenacious
thinking
thorough
thoughtful
thrifty
thriving
tolerant
tough
trusting
trustworthy
unassuming
understanding
unwavering
uplifting
useful
valuable
verbal
vibrant
wholesome
willing

Look through the "Personal Quality Words," and write which five adjectives would be used to describe you. (If you don't know, ask.)

My personal qualities according to my mother:

1. ______________________________
2. ______________________________
3. ______________________________
4. ______________________________
5. ______________________________

My personal qualities according to my father:

1. ______________________________
2. ______________________________
3. ______________________________
4. ______________________________
5. ______________________________

My personal qualities according to my friends:

1. ______________________________
2. ______________________________
3. ______________________________
4. ______________________________
5. ______________________________

My personal qualities according to me:

1. ______________________________
2. ______________________________
3. ______________________________
4. ______________________________
5. ______________________________

If asked to write a paper about yourself, what three topics would you feel best discussing?

1. ______________________ 2. ______________________ 3. ______________________

Make a list of the three most important events in your life. Why are they important to you?

1. Important Event 1 ____

Why was this event important to you? ____

2. Important Event 2 ____

Why was this event important to you? ____

3. Important Event 3 ____

Why was this event important to you? ____

If you are required to give a speech, what three topics would you choose?

1. ______________________________

2. ______________________________

3. ______________________________

List three people you most admire. Write why you admire them.

1. ______________________________

____

____

____

____

____

2. ______________________________

____

____

____

____

____

3. ______________________________

____

____

____

____

____

Who are your favorite bands or musicians?

1. ______________________________
2. ______________________________
3. ______________________________

What are your three favorite books you've read that were not assigned in school?

1. ______________________________
2. ______________________________
3. ______________________________

What are your three favorite video games you play?

1. ______________________________
2. ______________________________
3. ______________________________

What are your three favorite TV shows that you watch?

1. ______________________________
2. ______________________________
3. ______________________________

What are your three favorite movies?

1. ______________________________
2. ______________________________
3. ______________________________

What are your three favorite memories from as early as you can remember?

1.

2. ____

3.

Which three people have influenced you the most? In what ways?

1. ______________________________

2.

3.

What is your favorite quotation? Describe what it means to you.

What is your favorite word? Why is it your favorite?

Interests, Achievements, and Skills Colleges Are Looking for
Where Do YOU Fit in?

Student Interests

1. Leadership
2. World view
3. Public speaker
4. Fiction writer
5. Science and awards
6. Entrepreneurial (business interests)
7. Intellectual curiosity (reads a lot, asks a lot of questions)
8. Performing arts (document participation in music, theatre, visual arts, dance)
9. Community service
10. Animal and plant experiences
11. Changing the world experience (climate change, human rights)
12. Sports and achievement

If the above interests do not sound like you, add your own personal interests. Choose the three personal interests that sound most like you. Write a half page to document your choices, giving examples of your school or out-of-school activities to show your point. For example:

1. Leadership:
I am Vice President of my high school class, team leader of my soccer team, church leader in our youth program, 1st violin in community orchestra.

2. World view:
I selected two foreign languages to study, watch international news online, occasionally read international newspapers, and watch foreign TV and movies.

4. Public speaker:
I do well in debate class. I won the English Language Competition and was selected to speak for our class at an all-school math competition. I ran for student government and presented my ideas in school assembly for three consecutive years.

1. ______________________________

____

____

____

____

____

____

____

____

____

2. ____

3. ____

Review all of your answers before you go on to the Campus Culture Quiz on the next page.

Campus Culture

Who is this kid behind that GPA and those TOEFL, IELTS, SAT, or ACT scores?

The colleges want to know. You want to know!

Think about your family, friends, school, and activity interests and how you spend your time. With your understanding of who you are as a student, daughter or son, friend, country's citizen, volunteer, athlete, musician, or artist, take the Campus Culture Quiz to start thinking about what kind of college will be the best match for who you are.

Talking to a sophomore at the University of Maryland, the young man explained, "I enrolled for the architecture program, and they dropped it for financial reasons my first semester."
"Why didn't you transfer?"
"Because I love it here!"

Students leave college because they don't fit in. They stay because it's a great match, the place where they can relax enough to feel confident as they live and learn at their best. Where will you fit in? What's the best college culture for you and the person you want to be?

10-Step Campus Culture Quiz

Take this 10-Step Quiz and find your match. Choose one answer for each question. Then fill out the key on page 19.

Step 1: What is your favorite school club or activity?
- a. SAT prep group
- b. environmental club
- c. sports
- d. philosophy club
- e. music or drama club

Step 2: You're planning Friday night with your friends. Where do you go?
- a. A friend's party
- b. USA-exchange student program
- c. high school arts festival
- d. science fair workshop
- e. climate-change film

Step 3: What was or is your favorite subject in junior year?
- a. art, music, or dance class
- b. chemistry or physics
- c. psychology, economics
- d. history
- e. literature

Step 4: What kind of student are you?
- a. I like to read and discuss in small study groups everything an author writes.
- b. I like time and space to try new mediums and designs for my ideas.
- c. I like to study in the library until I really understand my homework before I relax.
- d. I like to do my homework and leave plenty of time to work on my community service projects.
- e. I study my favorite subjects and don't mind winging it once in a while for the rest.

Step 5: What's your favorite sport or recreational activity?
a. the gym: treadmill, rowing machine, weights
b. biking, kayaking, camping out
c. team sports: soccer, basketball, rugby, volleyball
d. tennis, swimming, gym fitness activities
e. yoga, dance

Step 6: What do you consider your best quality to highlight on your college application?
a. curiosity
b. imagination
c. work ethic
d. compassion
e. loyalty

Step 7: When you daydream about Saturday night at college, what will you be doing?
a. fund-raising for a water purification group
b. cheering for the basketball team
c. attending a philosophy lecture
d. attending a philharmonic concert
e. attending an engineering internship program

Step 8: You are filling out your housing form for college. Where will you want to live?
a. freshman dormitory
b. theme house on campus
c. fraternity or sorority house on campus
d. living and learning center on campus
e. downtown apartment

Step 9: Imagine walking on campus and it begins to snow, what are you talking about?
a. the ski report for Saturday
b. the Jean-Paul Sartre film on Saturday
c. the winter photography show
d. selling pizzas in the dorms for all of the snow-bounds this weekend
e. the extra help needed at the soup kitchen this weekend

Step 10: What kind of friends do you hope to have when you get to college?
a. innovative friends who like to go to performances and art galleries
b. serious friends who are in college to get ahead in the world
c. friends who take action for social justice
d. friends who show up at the games and know how to have a good time
e. friends would rather socialize with a few than party with a crowd

KEY

Circle each letter you chose for all ten questions. Go down each vertical color column, starting with question one through question ten, and give yourself ten points for each letter that you chose. Add them up! Let's say you have 7 red, 2 gold, and 1 blue. That would be 70 % Collegiate, 20% Preprofessional, and 10% Creative . Match your scores with the College Culture descriptions on the next page.

	Red	**Purple**	**Blue**	**Gold**	**Green**
1.	c	d	e	a	b
2.	a	b	c	d	e
3.	d	e	a	b	c
4.	e	a	b	c	d
5.	c	d	e	a	b
6.	e	a	b	c	d
7.	b	c	d	e	a
8.	c	d	e	a	b
9.	a	b	c	d	e
10.	d	e	a	b	c

College Culture Descriptions

Red **Collegiate** college culture such as the University of Michigan, Duke, Northwestern, Georgetown, Penn State, Vanderbilt, or smaller campuses such as Colgate, Denison, and Wake Forest. A college culture where you will find big sports, fraternities, and where you will talk about sports, parties, and friends between classes and in the dorms.

Purple **Intellectual** college culture such as Swarthmore, Chicago, Grinnell, Pomona, and Carlton where you and your friends will spend your time talking about books you've read, where you will continue your discussions from class, argue and debate about academics, politics, and economics.

Blue **Creative** college culture for design and performing arts majors such as conservatories Julliard, Lawrence University and Oberlin or design schools such as Rhode Island School of Design or Savannah School of Arts and Design where you and your friends will talk and sing between classes and in the dorms about the arts, practice sessions, gallery openings, fashion, and upcoming performances.

Gold **Preprofessional** college culture where you and your friends talk between classes and in the dorms about GPAs, MCATs, GREs, LSATs, M.B.A.s, start-up companies, Jeff Bezos, the global economy, medical and law school, business, engineering, and architecture schools, such as Carnegie Mellon, Cornell, Purdue, UNC, the University of Rochester, RPI, Wharton, George Washington University, University of Illinois, and Northeastern.

Green **Activist** college culture where you and your friends will protest, organize, demonstrate, boycott, and talk about human rights, animal rights, environmental, and climate issues between classes, in the dorms, and on the quad such as Grinnell, Haverford, Oberlin, Pitzer, and Wesleyan.

How did you do? Are you strongest in Collegiate? Second in Preprofessional? Is an Activist culture important to you? Remember that these categories are determined by what students talk about outside of the classroom–at meals, between classes, in the dorm, in the locker room, in the student union, at games, having a coffee, in the library, and everywhere you go. College culture is the heart of student life on campus.

Think about it. Does it make sense? With your best college cultures match in mind, you are now ready to research the colleges with the most "you" in the college culture as an important ingredient of how you choose where you will apply to go to college. The more you know about your match, the better college list you will have–leading to the best college choice for you. The colleges all want to know why you think that their college is a good fit for you. Knowing each college culture will be your best bet!

Part II
Searching the Colleges–Building Your College List

The College Market Is not a Tight Market.

There are hundreds of four-year accredited colleges with different campus cultures and high academic standards all over America. You would like many of them if only you knew more about them. In fact, there are more than 2,500 residential, accredited four-year degree-granting colleges in the USA. Every one of those colleges is wonderful for someone. Not one of them is wonderful for everyone. Some students find it so difficult to get in simply because they think that only a few are the best for them–the ones that they have heard of from their family or neighbors or friends. Knowing where the graduating classes from your school go to college is one way to begin your college list. Ask your school counselor where students with your academic record were accepted and enrolled, realizing that these colleges will take a few from any one high school. The purpose of this book is to get you to think about who you are as a student and person, to learn a lot more about the great variety of college choices, and to write an application for the colleges that will be wonderful for you. For example, families may have heard very little about some of America's most intellectual colleges: University of Chicago, Swarthmore, Pomona, and Carleton. Most engineering students know about MIT, and yet, just as selective for engineering, mathematics, and physics are California College of Technology (Cal Tech) Harvey Mudd, Olin College, RPI, Georgia Tech, and Purdue. This book will help you to search what's out there–so that you will have the best choices for who you are as a student–because it is not a tight market!

To get you some college choices in April of your junior year or December of your senior year, you are going to learn how to go beyond the college rankings and the few colleges that you have heard of. A special problem for students is that they think that rankings means what's best for them, so they all apply to the same few colleges. In other words, students tend to think alike rather than realizing that there are many other colleges for different personalities of students. For example, think about cars… the car of choice in China is the Audi, so everyone wants an Audi. In America, many students would want a Ford pick-up truck, an open Jeep, or a little VW Beatle convertible. There wouldn't be "one" that is the best for everyone… not cars, or colleges, watches, or jeans. When April of senior year comes around, and college decisions are sent out, you will want to have thought through a wide range of school choices during the previous year. The purpose of building your college list is to use this book to think about what it is that you like–what's best for you–and then to search for ten or twelve colleges that vary in selectivity and to be sure that you would go to each one where you apply. If you do your search well, and you learn to write an application and essay that is unique, you won't sound like every other student, "I only want to go to a college I've heard of."

What is the College Dean of Admissions looking for to admit a student to her/his college? The dean is looking for someone who has something special to bring to this particular campus. A student who writes about and will talk about the politics, history, art, and literature that he likes or she doesn't like. A student who wants to play in the college band or plays sports or loves snowboarding. Someone who asks great questions and knows things. Someone who reads books not required. Someone with courage to learn and try new things. A student who will add diversity to the campus because of the school they are from, or state, or interest they have, or one who wants to start something new on campus.

You are going to learn about and fill out 20 college worksheets in this book to build your list. Finally, by September of senior year, you will choose your final 10 and apply to each one. You will find these 20 colleges from college guides, your friends, online searches, college fairs, college events, college tours, and some colleges may just drop out of the air in your dreams!

Building Your College List

Buy a U.S. college guide online or in your local bookstore; *The Fiske Guide to Colleges or The Ultimate Guide to America's Best Colleges* are both good. Don't even think about building your college list of 20 or writing your applications without one of these two descriptive guides to American colleges.

Why? Because these two guides describe what you need to know about living and learning at the particular college. They are written by educators, not admissions people selling their own college, not students loyal to their own experience, and not online, where the college website is very valuable but their purpose is to sell their college.

This book has a separate worksheet for each college you research. You will get the information you need to build your college list of 20 from more than 350 residential colleges. You will learn enough about 20 colleges to write a strong application, and to choose your final college list of eight to ten colleges to which to apply.

Don't skip this exercise because no one else has bothered with reading the guides about the hundreds of fabulous opportunities you will find in America! Don't skip it because you have never heard of the colleges. Don't skip it because you want only what everyone else wants. Search the college guides because you have the courage to learn about places you have never heard of, possibly colleges that are just right for YOU!

Step 1: Search college guides–think and write in your College Search Worksheets
With a college guide in hand, read about three colleges that you already know from hearing their names from family and friends. Next, read about three colleges you probably have never heard of–filling in your College Search Worksheet as colleges numbers 4, 5, and 6. Numbers 7, 8, and 9 are three state universities that you may not know. For each of the colleges, you will need one of the college guides to fill in what you learn and then think about and write your own personal opinion of the college. At the end of the college description in your college guide, there is always a list of three or more "overlaps." Overlaps are colleges where students also applied, usually because it is a similar college. It's a good way to build your college list. Check out the overlaps of colleges that sound like a possible choice for you. When you find an overlap that you like, add that college to your list in the last blank of your worksheets. You may also want to add colleges to your list of 20 that sound interesting to you from college fairs, online searches, or friends who are college students to build your list of 20 colleges.

Step 2: Search online for colleges–think and fill in your College Search Worksheets
You have a list of colleges from your College search woorksheets. If you don't yet have 20 colleges, and you are a junior, you have plenty of time to learn more about interesting colleges before you need your final list. If you are a senior and need a longer list, go back to the colleges on your Worksheets that sound best to you and read about each of their overlaps. Choose overlaps to fill in your worksheets from which you will choose your final list of 8 to 10 colleges. Start with the most interesting colleges you have recorded on your worksheets, and search online for their websites. Look at Campus Life, Student Publications, Residential Life, Dining Facilities, Student Organizations, and anything that interests you on their websites. Check out academic requirements and numbers of residential students. Whatever you find that you like or don't like, find a place on your College Search Worksheet to write what you've learned online. Looking at a college website, find the name and email address of your school's admissions officer, that is, the representative (the rep) for your particular high school, city, state, or country. Colleges vary in how they break down admissions responsibilities…but know this…there isn't a school on the globe that doesn't have someone in the college admissions office responsible for your high school! Write the name and email address of this person in this workbook so that you can be in touch if you decide to apply.

Students like to search colleges online at many sites. Some of these websites have personal choices for you to fill in about your academic record and interests, and then the site comes up with a list of colleges. After starting your list from the college guides, you can compare your list to the online lists projected for you. You will make your final list of what makes most sense to you–don't let an impersonal online website make decisions for you! Two favorites of American students are the College Board (www.collegeboard.com) and the Princeton Review (www.review.com). Add any new colleges that you find interesting to your College Search Worksheets. Use the back of the Workbook's extra pages for College Notes to keep a record of colleges that you like and want to add to your search list.

College Search Worksheets

Three Colleges I Have Heard Of

Student Choice 1: ______________________________

Address of college: ______________________________

____

Web address: ______________________________

Student Body

Number of undergraduates: ____________________

Number of graduates: ____________________

Male/female ratio: ____________________

International student percentage: ____________________

Residence

Freshmen on campus: ____________________

Upperclassmen on campus: ____________________

Commuters from home: ____________________

Off-campus apartments: ____________________

Academics

Average GPA: ____________________

Average SAT/ACT: ____________________

Average TOEFL or IELTS score: ____________________

Average class size: ____________________

Popular majors: ____________________

Writing support: ____________________

Academic advising support: ____________________

Extracurricular Opportunities

Political clubs: ______________________________

____

Foreign-language clubs: ______________________________

____

Newspaper, publication clubs: ______________________________

____

Other clubs: ______________________________

____

Athletics (varsity, intramurals, club, dormitory): ______________________________

____

Cultural events: ______________________________

____

____

Community service opportunities: ______________________________

____

____

Other activities that interest me: ______________________________

____

____

What I Learned About This College

What I like about it: ______________________________

What I don't like about it: ______________________________

What I will look up to learn more: ______________________________

Decisions: Definite NO! ______ Learn more: ______ Add to possible list of 20 colleges: ______

Student Choice 2: ______________________________

Address of college: ______________________________

____

Web address: ______________________________

Student Body

Number of undergraduates: ____________________

Number of graduates: ____________________

Male/female ratio: ____________________

International student percentage: ____________________

Residence

Freshmen on campus: ____________________

Upperclassmen on campus: ____________________

Commuters from home: ____________________

Off-campus apartments: ____________________

Academics

Average GPA: ____________________

Average SAT/ACT: ____________________

Average TOEFL or IELTS score: ____________________

Average class size: ____________________

Popular majors: ____________________

Writing support: ____________________

Academic advising support: ____________________

Extracurricular Opportunities

Political clubs: ______________________________

____

Foreign-language clubs: ______________________________

____

Newspaper, publication clubs: ______________________________

____

Other clubs: ______________________________

____

Athletics (varsity, intramurals, club, dormitory): ______________________________

____

Cultural events: ______________________________

____

____

Community service opportunities: ______________________________

____

____

Other activities that interest me: ______________________________

____

____

What I Learned About This College

What I like about it: ____________________

____

____

____

____

____

____

____

____

____

What I don't like about it: ____________________

____

____

____

____

____

____

____

____

____

What I will look up to learn more: ____________________

____

____

Decisions: Definite NO! ______ Learn more: ______ Add to possible list of 20 colleges: ______

Student Choice 3: ______________________________

Address of college: ______________________________

____

Web address: ______________________________

Student Body

Number of undergraduates: ____________________

Number of graduates: ____________________

Male/female ratio: ____________________

International student percentage: ____________________

Residence

Freshmen on campus: ____________________

Upperclassmen on campus: ____________________

Commuters from home: ____________________

Off-campus apartments: ____________________

Academics

Average GPA: ____________________

Average SAT/ACT: ____________________

Average TOEFL or IELTS score: ____________________

Average class size: ____________________

Popular majors: ____________________

Writing support: ____________________

Academic advising support: ____________________

Extracurricular Opportunities

Political clubs: ______________________________

____

Foreign-language clubs: ______________________________

____

Newspaper, publication clubs: ______________________________

____

Other clubs: ______________________________

____

Athletics (varsity, intramurals, club, dormitory): ______________________________

____

Cultural events: ______________________________

____

____

Community service opportunities: ______________________________

____

____

Other activities that interest me: ______________________________

____

____

What I Learned About This College

What I like about it: ____________________

____

____

____

____

____

____

____

____

____

What I don't like about it: ____________________

____

____

____

____

____

____

____

____

____

What I will look up to learn more: ____________________

____

____

Decisions: Definite NO! ______ Learn more: ______ Add to possible list of 20 colleges: ______

Three Colleges I Know Very Little About

With College guide in hand – look up and read about these three colleges that you may know little about: Goucher College, Macalester College, and Occidental College.

Goucher College

Address of college: ______________________________

____

Web address: ______________________________

Student Body

Number of undergraduates: ____________________

Number of graduates: ____________________

Male/female ratio: ____________________

International student percentage: ____________________

Residence

Freshmen on campus: ____________________

Upperclassmen on campus: ____________________

Commuters from home: ____________________

Off-campus apartments: ____________________

Academics

Average GPA: ____________________

Average SAT/ACT: ____________________

Average TOEFL or IELTS score: ____________________

Average class size: ____________________

Popular majors: ____________________

Writing support: ____________________

Academic advising support: ____________________

Extracurricular Opportunities

Political clubs: ______________________________

____

Foreign-language clubs: ______________________________

____

Newspaper, publication clubs: ______________________________

____

Other clubs: ______________________________

____

Athletics (varsity, intramurals, club, dormitory): ______________________________

____

Cultural events: ______________________________

____

____

Community service opportunities: ______________________________

____

____

Other activities that interest me: ______________________________

____

____

What I Learned About This College

What I like about it: ____

____

____

____

____

____

____

____

____

____

What I don't like about it: ____

____

____

____

____

____

____

____

____

____

What I will look up to learn more: ____

____

____

Decisions: Definite NO! ______ Learn more: ______ Add to possible list of 20 colleges: ______

Macalester College

Address of college: ______________________________

____

Web address: ______________________________

Student Body

Number of undergraduates: ______________

Number of graduates: ______________

Male/female ratio: ______________

International student percentage: ______________

Residence

Freshmen on campus: ______________

Upperclassmen on campus: ______________

Commuters from home: ______________

Off-campus apartments: ______________

Academics

Average GPA: ______________

Average SAT/ACT: ______________

Average TOEFL or IELTS score: ______________

Average class size: ______________

Popular majors: ______________

Writing support: ______________

Academic advising support: ______________

Extracurricular Opportunities

Political clubs: ____

____

Foreign-language clubs: ____

____

Newspaper, publication clubs: ____

____

Other clubs: ____

____

Athletics (varsity, intramurals, club, dormitory): ____

____

Cultural events: ____

____

____

Community service opportunities: ____

____

____

Other activities that interest me: ____

____

____

What I Learnec About This College

What I like about it: ____________________

____

____

____

____

____

____

____

____

____

What I don't like about it: ____________________

____

____

____

____

____

____

____

____

____

What I will look up to learn more: ____________________

____

____

Decisions: Definite NO! ______ Learn more: ______ Add to possible list of 20 colleges: ______

Occidental College

Address of college: ______________________________

____

Web address: ______________________________

Student Body

Number of undergraduates: ____________________

Number of graduates: ____________________

Male/female ratio: ____________________

International student percentage: ____________________

Residence

Freshmen on campus: ____________________

Upperclassmen on campus: ____________________

Commuters from home: ____________________

Off-campus apartments: ____________________

Academics

Average GPA: ____________________

Average SAT/ACT: ____________________

Average TOEFL or IELTS score: ____________________

Average class size: ____________________

Popular majors: ____________________

Writing support: ____________________

Academic advising support: ____________________

Extracurricular Opportunities

Political clubs: ____

____

Foreign-language clubs: ____

____

Newspaper, publication clubs: ____

____

Other clubs: ____

____

Athletics (varsity, intramurals, club, dormitory): ____

____

Cultural events: ____

____

____

Community service opportunities: ____

____

____

Other activities that interest me: ____

____

____

What I Learned About This College

What I like about it: ____

____

____

____

____

____

____

____

____

____

What I don't like about it: ____

____

____

____

____

____

____

____

____

____

What I will look up to learn more: ____

____

____

Decisions: Definite NO! ______ Learn more: ______ Add to possible list of 20 colleges: ______

State Universities

Read about three state universities in your college guide that you have not yet heard much about: University of Mississippi, Montana State University, and the University of Vermont.

University of Mississippi

Address of college: ______________________________

____

Web address: ______________________________

Student Body

Number of undergraduates: ______________________________

Number of graduates: ______________________________

Male/female ratio: ______________________________

International student percentage: ______________________________

Residence

Freshmen on campus: ______________________________

Upperclassmen on campus: ______________________________

Commuters from home: ______________________________

Off-campus apartments: ______________________________

Academics

Average GPA: ______________________________

Average SAT/ACT: ______________________________

Average TOEFL or IELTS score: ______________________________

Average class size: ______________________________

Popular majors: ______________________________

Writing support: ______________________________

Academic advising support: ______________________________

Extracurricular Opportunities

Political clubs: ____

____

Foreign-language clubs: ____

____

Newspaper, publication clubs: ____

____

Other clubs: ____

____

Athletics (varsity, intramurals, club, dormitory): ____

____

Cultural events: ____

____

____

Community service opportunities: ____

____

____

Other activities that interest me: ____

____

____

What I Learned About This College

What I like about it: ____

____

____

____

____

____

____

____

____

____

What I don't like about it: ____

____

____

____

____

____

____

____

____

____

What I will look up to learn more: ____

____

____

Decisions: Definite NO! ______ Learn more: ______ Add to possible list of 20 colleges: ______

Montana State University

Address of college: ______________________________

____

Web address: ______________________________

Student Body

Number of undergraduates: ____________________

Number of graduates: ____________________

Male/female ratio: ____________________

International student percentage: ____________________

Residence

Freshmen on campus: ____________________

Upperclassmen on campus: ____________________

Commuters from home: ____________________

Off-campus apartments: ____________________

Academics

Average GPA: ____________________

Average SAT/ACT: ____________________

Average TOEFL or IELTS score: ____________________

Average class size: ____________________

Popular majors: ____________________

Writing support: ____________________

Academic advising support: ____________________

Extracurricular Opportunities

Political clubs: ______________________________

____

Foreign-language clubs: ______________________________

____

Newspaper, publication clubs: ______________________________

____

Other clubs: ______________________________

____

Athletics (varsity, intramurals, club, dormitory): ______________________________

____

Cultural events: ______________________________

____

____

Community service opportunities: ______________________________

____

____

Other activities that interest me: ______________________________

____

____

What I Learned About This College

What I like about it: ______________________________

____

____

____

____

____

____

____

____

____

What I don't like about it: ______________________________

____

____

____

____

____

____

____

____

____

What I will look up to learn more: ______________________________

____

____

Decisions: Defin te NO! ______ Learn more: ______ Add to possible list of 20 colleges: ______

University of Vermont

Address of college: ______________________________

____

Web address: ______________________________

Student Body

Number of undergraduates: ______________

Number of graduates: ______________

Male/female ratio: ______________

International student percentage: ______________

Residence

Freshmen on campus: ______________

Upperclassmen on campus: ______________

Commuters from home: ______________

Off-campus apartments: ______________

Academics

Average GPA: ______________

Average SAT/ACT: ______________

Average TOEFL or IELTS score: ______________

Average class size: ______________

Popular majors: ______________

Writing support: ______________

Academic advising support: ______________

Extracurricular Opportunities

Political clubs: ______________________________

____

Foreign-language clubs: ______________________________

____

Newspaper, publication clubs: ______________________________

____

Other clubs: ______________________________

____

Athletics (varsity, intramurals, club, dormitory): ______________________________

____

Cultural events: ______________________________

____

____

Community service opportunities: ______________________________

____

____

Other activities that interest me: ______________________________

____

____

What I Learned About This College

What I like about it: ____________________

____

____

____

____

____

____

____

____

____

What I don't like about it: ____________________

____

____

____

____

____

____

____

____

____

What I will look up to learn more: ____________________

____

____

Decisions: Definite NO! ______ Learn more: ______ Add to possible list of 20 colleges: ______

Eleven More Colleges

College 10: ____________________

Address of college: ____________________

____

Web address: ____________________

Student Body

Number of undergraduates: ____________________

Number of graduates: ____________________

Male/female ratio: ____________________

International student percentage: ____________________

Residence

Freshmen on campus: ____________________

Upperclassmen on campus: ____________________

Commuters from home: ____________________

Off-campus apartments: ____________________

Academics

Average GPA: ____________________

Average SAT/ACT: ____________________

Average TOEFL or IELTS score: ____________________

Average class size: ____________________

Popular majors: ____________________

Writing support: ____________________

Academic advising support: ____________________

Extracurricular Opportunities

Political clubs: ____

____

Foreign-language clubs: ____

____

Newspaper, publication clubs: ____

____

Other clubs: ____

____

Athletics (varsity, intramurals, club, dormitory): ____

____

Cultural events: ____

____

____

Community service opportunities: ____

____

____

Other activities that interest me: ____

____

____

What I Learned About This College

What I like about it: ______________________________

____

____

____

____

____

____

____

____

____

What I don't like about it: ______________________________

____

____

____

____

____

____

____

____

____

What I will look up to learn more: ______________________________

____

____

Decisions: Definite NO! ______ Learn more: ______ Add to possible list of 20 colleges: ______

College 11: ____________________

Address of college: ____________________

____

Web address: ____________________

Student Body

Number of undergraduates: ____________________

Number of graduates: ____________________

Male/female ratio: ____________________

International student percentage: ____________________

Residence

Freshmen on campus: ____________________

Upperclassmen on campus: ____________________

Commuters from home: ____________________

Off-campus apartments: ____________________

Academics

Average GPA: ____________________

Average SAT/ACT: ____________________

Average TOEFL or IELTS score: ____________________

Average class size: ____________________

Popular majors: ____________________

Writing support: ____________________

Academic advising support: ____________________

Extracurricular Opportunities

Political clubs: ______________________________

____

Foreign-language clubs: ______________________________

____

Newspaper, publication clubs: ______________________________

____

Other clubs: ______________________________

____

Athletics (varsity, intramurals, club, dormitory): ______________________________

____

Cultural events: ______________________________

____

____

Community service opportunities: ______________________________

____

____

Other activities that interest me: ______________________________

____

____

What I Learned About This College

What I like about it: ____

____

____

____

____

____

____

____

____

____

What I don't like about it: ____

____

____

____

____

____

____

____

____

____

What I will look up to learn more: ____

____

____

Decisions: Definite NO! _______ Learn more: _______ Add to possible list of 20 colleges: _______

College 12: ____________________

Address of college: ____________________

____

Web address: ____________________

Student Body

Number of undergraduates: ____________________

Number of graduates: ____________________

Male/female ratio: ____________________

International student percentage: ____________________

Residence

Freshmen on campus: ____________________

Upperclassmen on campus: ____________________

Commuters from home: ____________________

Off-campus apartments: ____________________

Academics

Average GPA: ____________________

Average SAT/ACT: ____________________

Average TOEFL or IELTS score: ____________________

Average class size: ____________________

Popular majors: ____________________

Writing support: ____________________

Academic advising support: ____________________

Extracurricular Opportunities

Political clubs: ______________________________

____

Foreign-language clubs: ______________________________

____

Newspaper, publication clubs: ______________________________

____

Other clubs: ______________________________

____

Athletics (varsity, intramurals, club, dormitory): ______________________________

____

Cultural events: ______________________________

____

____

Community service opportunities: ______________________________

____

____

Other activities that interest me: ______________________________

____

____

What I Learned About This College

What I like about it: ____

____

____

____

____

____

____

____

____

____

What I don't like about it: ____

____

____

____

____

____

____

____

____

____

What I will look up to learn more: ____

____

____

Decisions: Definite NO! ______ Learn more: ______ Add to possible list of 20 colleges: ______

College 13: ______________________________

Address of college: ______________________________

____

Web address: ______________________________

Student Body

Number of undergraduates: ______________

Number of graduates: ______________

Male/female ratio: ______________

International student percentage: ______________

Residence

Freshmen on campus: ______________

Upperclassmen on campus: ______________

Commuters from home: ______________

Off-campus apartments: ______________

Academics

Average GPA: ______________

Average SAT/ACT: ______________

Average TOEFL or IELTS score: ______________

Average class size: ______________

Popular majors: ______________

Writing support: ______________

Academic advising support: ______________

Extracurricular Opportunities

Political clubs: ______________________________

____

Foreign-language clubs: ______________________________

____

Newspaper, publication clubs: ______________________________

____

Other clubs: ______________________________

____

Athletics (varsity, intramurals, club, dormitory): ______________________________

____

Cultural events: ______________________________

____

____

Community service opportunities: ______________________________

____

____

Other activities that interest me: ______________________________

____

____

What I Learned About This College

What I like about it: ______________________________

What I don't like about it: ______________________________

What I will look up to learn more: ______________________________

Decisions: Definite NO! ______ Learn more: ______ Add to possible list of 20 colleges: ______

College 14: ____________________

Address of college: ____________________

____

Web address: ____________________

Student Body

Number of undergraduates: ____________________

Number of graduates: ____________________

Male/female ratio: ____________________

International student percentage: ____________________

Residence

Freshmen on campus: ____________________

Upperclassmen on campus: ____________________

Commuters from home: ____________________

Off-campus apartments: ____________________

Academics

Average GPA: ____________________

Average SAT/ACT: ____________________

Average TOEFL or IELTS score: ____________________

Average class size: ____________________

Popular majors: ____________________

Writing support: ____________________

Academic advising support: ____________________

Extracurricular Opportunities

Political clubs: ____________________

____

Foreign-language clubs: ____________________

____

Newspaper, publication clubs: ____________________

____

Other clubs: ____________________

____

Athletics (varsity, intramurals, club, dormitory): ____________________

____

Cultural events: ____________________

____

____

Community service opportunities: ____________________

____

____

Other activities that interest me: ____________________

____

____

What I Learned About This College

What I like about it: ____

____

____

____

____

____

____

____

____

____

What I don't like about it: ____

____

____

____

____

____

____

____

____

____

What I will look up to learn more: ____

____

____

Decisions: Definite NO! ______ Learn more: ______ Add to possible list of 20 colleges: ______

College 15: ______________________________

Address of college: ______________________________

____

Web address: ______________________________

Student Body

Number of undergraduates: ______________

Number of graduates: ______________

Male/female ratio: ______________

International student percentage: ______________

Residence

Freshmen on campus: ______________

Upperclassmen on campus: ______________

Commuters from home: ______________

Off-campus apartments: ______________

Academics

Average GPA: ______________

Average SAT/ACT: ______________

Average TOEFL or IELTS score: ______________

Average class size: ______________

Popular majors: ______________

Writing support: ______________

Academic advising support: ______________

Extracurricular Opportunities

Political clubs: ______________________________

____

Foreign-language clubs: ______________________________

____

Newspaper, publication clubs: ______________________________

____

Other clubs: ______________________________

____

Athletics (varsity, intramurals, club, dormitory): ______________________________

____

Cultural events: ______________________________

____

____

Community service opportunities: ______________________________

____

____

Other activities that interest me: ______________________________

____

____

What I Learned About This College

What I like about it: ____

____

____

____

____

____

____

____

____

____

What I don't like about it: ____

____

____

____

____

____

____

____

____

____

What I will look up to learn more: ____

____

____

Decisions: Definite NO! _______ Learn more: _______ Add to possible list of 20 colleges: _______

College 16: ______________________________

Address of college: ______________________________

____

Web address: ______________________________

Student Body

Number of undergraduates: ____________________

Number of graduates: ____________________

Male/female ratio: ____________________

International student percentage: ____________________

Residence

Freshmen on campus: ____________________

Upperclassmen on campus: ____________________

Commuters from home: ____________________

Off-campus apartments: ____________________

Academics

Average GPA: ____________________

Average SAT/ACT: ____________________

Average TOEFL or IELTS score: ____________________

Average class size: ____________________

Popular majors: ____________________

Writing support: ____________________

Academic advising support: ____________________

Extracurricular Opportunities

Political clubs: ______________________________

____

Foreign-language clubs: ______________________________

____

Newspaper, publication clubs: ______________________________

____

Other clubs: ______________________________

____

Athletics (varsity, intramurals, club, dormitory): ______________________________

____

Cultural events: ______________________________

____

____

Community service opportunities: ______________________________

____

____

Other activities that interest me: ______________________________

____

____

What I Learned About This College

What I like about it: ____________________

____

____

____

____

____

____

____

____

____

What I don't like about it: ____________________

____

____

____

____

____

____

____

____

____

What I will look up to learn more: ____________________

____

____

Decisions: Definite NO! ______ Learn more: ______ Add to possible list of 20 colleges: ______

College 17: ____________________

Address of college: ____________________

____

Web address: ____________________

Student Body

Number of undergraduates: ____________________

Number of graduates: ____________________

Male/female ratio: ____________________

International student percentage: ____________________

Residence

Freshmen on campus: ____________________

Upperclassmen on campus: ____________________

Commuters from home: ____________________

Off_campus apartments: ____________________

Academics

Average GPA: ____________________

Average SAT/ACT: ____________________

Average TOEFL or IELTS score: ____________________

Average class size: ____________________

Popular majors: ____________________

Writing support: ____________________

Academic advising support: ____________________

Extracurricular Opportunities

Political clubs: ____________________

____

Foreign-language clubs: ____________________

____

Newspaper, publication clubs: ____________________

____

Other clubs: ____________________

____

Athletics (varsity, intramurals, club, dormitory): ____________________

____

Cultural events: ____________________

____

____

Community service opportunities: ____________________

____

____

Other activities that interest me: ____________________

____

____

What I Learned About This College

What I like about it: ______________________________

What I don't like about it: ______________________________

What I will look up to learn more: ______________________________

Decisions: Definite NO! ______ Learn more: ______ Add to possible list of 20 colleges: ______

College 18: ______________________________

Address of college: ______________________________

____

Web address: ______________________________

Student Body

Number of undergraduates: ____________________

Number of graduates: ____________________

Male/female ratio: ____________________

International student percentage: ____________________

Residence

Freshmen on campus: ____________________

Upperclassmen on campus: ____________________

Commuters from home: ____________________

Off-campus apartments: ____________________

Academics

Average GPA: ____________________

Average SAT/ACT: ____________________

Average TOEFL or IELTS score: ____________________

Average class size: ____________________

Popular majors: ____________________

Writing support: ____________________

Academic advising support: ____________________

Extracurricular Opportunities

Political clubs: ____

____

Foreign-language clubs: ____

____

Newspaper, publication clubs: ____

____

Other clubs: ____

____

Athletics (varsity, intramurals, club, dormitory): ____

____

Cultural events: ____

____

____

Community service opportunities: ____

____

____

Other activities that interest me: ____

____

____

What I Learned About This College

What I like about it: ______________________________________

____

____

____

____

____

____

____

____

____

What I don't like about it: ______________________________________

____

____

____

____

____

____

____

____

____

What I will look up to learn more: ______________________________________

____

____

Decisions: Definite NO! ______ Learn more: ______ Add to possible list of 20 colleges: ______

College 19: ______________________________

Address of college: ______________________________

____

Web address: ______________________________

Student Body

Number of undergraduates: ______________________________

Number of graduates: ______________________________

Male/female ratio: ______________________________

International student percentage: ______________________________

Residence

Freshmen on campus: ______________________________

Upperclassmen on campus: ______________________________

Commuters from home: ______________________________

Off-campus apartments: ______________________________

Academics

Average GPA: ______________________________

Average SAT/ACT: ______________________________

Average TOEFL or IELTS score: ______________________________

Average class size: ______________________________

Popular majors: ______________________________

Writing support: ______________________________

Academic advising support: ______________________________

Extracurricular Opportunities

Political clubs: ____

____

Foreign-language clubs: ____

____

Newspaper, publication clubs: ____

____

Other clubs: ____

____

Athletics (varsity, intramurals, club, dormitory): ____

____

Cultural events: ____

____

____

Community service opportunities: ____

____

____

Other activities that interest me: ____

____

____

What I Learned About This College

What I like about it: ____

____

____

____

____

____

____

____

____

____

What I don't like about it: ____

____

____

____

____

____

____

____

____

____

What I will look up to learn more: ____

____

____

Decisions: Definite NO! ______ Learn more: ______ Add to possible list of 20 colleges: ______

College 20: ______________________________

Address of college: ______________________________

____

Web address: ______________________________

Student Body

Number of undergraduates: ______________________

Number of graduates: ______________________

Male/female ratio: ______________________

International student percentage: ______________________

Residence

Freshmen on campus: ______________________

Upperclassmen on campus: ______________________

Commuters from home: ______________________

Off-campus apartments: ______________________

Academics

Average GPA: ______________________

Average SAT/ACT: ______________________

Average TOEFL or IELTS score: ______________________

Average class size: ______________________

Popular majors: ______________________

Writing support: ______________________

Academic advising support: ______________________

Extracurricular Opportunities

Political clubs: ______________________________

____

Foreign-language clubs: ______________________________

____

Newspaper, publication clubs: ______________________________

____

Other clubs: ______________________________

____

Athletics (varsity, intramurals, club, dormitory): ______________________________

____

Cultural events: ______________________________

____

____

Community service opportunities: ______________________________

____

____

Other activities that interest me: ______________________________

____

____

What I Learned About This College

What I like about it: ____________________

What I don't like about it: ____________________

What I will look up to learn more: ____________________

Decisions: Definite NO! ______ Learn more: ______ Add to possible list of 20 colleges: ______

Search College Fairs

Step 3: Search college fairs–think and fill in your College Fair Worksheets
Every year there are more college fairs being held in the major US cities and high schools as well as cities all over the world. About ten years ago, U.S. colleges started flocking to mainland China where fairs were held in Shenzhen, Shanghai, and Beijing, and now they are in many more cities. If you are a junior or an expat in an international school, or you are an international student looking for an American college and you hear about an American college fair; be sure and go! These are usually college fairs for students and their parents. You will have a chance to talk to the admissions staff of the college. Most important, you will have an opportunity to ask questions! Before you go: 1. Read about the college in your College Guide, 2. Check out their website, and 3. Take along this book, your device, or paper and pen so that you can write about the different colleges you find at the fair. Take your backpack or book bag so that you have a place to put the college brochures from the colleges that interest you.

Even if you go with friends, don't stick together! You alone will be applying and you alone who will have questions that narrow your choices as you build your college list.

Questions to Ask the College Fair Rep

1. What is special about your college?
2. What are the most popular majors?
3. What are the most unique majors?
4. Do most students live on campus?
5. Do you have support staff for advising about which courses to take?
6. Where do freshman live?
7. What do students do on weekends?
8. Do you have fencing or badminton or rugby varsity sports teams?
9. Add your own special interest questions.

   a. ______________________________

   ____

   b. ______________________________

   ____

   c. ______________________________

   ____

After you talk to the admissions officer or an alumna (a graduate of that college),

1. Fill out the college card only if the college interests you.
2. Write your own notes for each college. Be sure you get the college rep's business card with her/his email address so that if the college interests you, you can write to thank her/him for the conversation you had at the fair.
3. If you like the college and plan to consider it for your final list, fill out the College Search Worksheet in this book when you get home.

College Fair Worksheets

College 1

Name of college: ______________________________

State: ____________

Name of admissions officer: ______________________________

What surprised me: ______________________________

____

Student housing on and off campus: ____________

Housing for freshman: ____________

Housing for upperclassmen: ____________

What impressed me the most: ______________________________

____

What clubs and activities interest me: ______________________________

Email address of a student whom I met on campus: ______________________________

To do: Check out college guide and website.

College 2

Name of college: ____

State: ______________

Name of admissions officer: ______________________________________

What surprised me: ____

____

Student housing on and off campus: ______________

Housing for freshman: ______________

Housing for upperclassmen: ______________

What impressed me the most: _____________________________________

____

What clubs and activities interest me: ____________________________

Email address of a student whom I met on campus: ___________________

To do: Check out college guide and website.

College 3

Name of college: ____

State: ____________

Name of admissions officer: ______________________________________

What surprised me: ____

____

Student housing on and off campus: ____________

Housing for freshman: ____________

Housing for upperclassmen: ____________

What impressed me the most: ______________________________________

____

What clubs and activities interest me: ______________________________

Email address of a student whom I met on campus: ___________________

To do: Check out college guide and website.

College 4

Name of college: ____________________

State: __________

Name of admissions officer: ____________________

What surprised me: ____________________

____

Student housing on and off campus: __________

Housing for freshman: __________

Housing for upperclassmen: __________

What impressed me the most: ____________________

____

What clubs and activities interest me: ____________________

Email address of a student whom I met on campus: ____________________

To do: Check out college guide and website.

College 5

Name of college: ______________________________

State: ____________

Name of admissions officer: ______________________________

What surprised me: ______________________________

____

Student housing on and off campus: ____________

Housing for freshman: ____________

Housing for upperclassmen: ____________

What impressed me the most: ______________________________

____

What clubs and activities interest me: ______________________________

Email address of a student whom I met on campus: ______________________________

To do: Check out college guide and website.

College 6

Name of college: ____

State: _______________

Name of admissions officer: ____

What surprised me: ____

____

Student housing on and off campus: _______________

Housing for freshman: _______________

Housing for upperclassmen: _______________

What impressed me the most: ____

____

What clubs and activities interest me: ____

Email address of a student whom I met on campus: ____

To do: Check out college guide and website.

Search College Presentations

Step 4: Search college presentations–think and fill in your College Presentation Worksheets
Each year finds more colleges giving presentations in a greater variety of U.S. and international cities, from Cleveland in the Midwest to L.A. and from Paris to Shanghai. Sometimes these presentations are organized by individual colleges and given by a graduate of the college; and other times a few colleges travel together, such as the "Sister Schools," that is, women's colleges: Barnard, Bryn Mawr, Mount Holyoke, Smith, and Wellesley. Sometimes a college counseling or test prep business will sponsor colleges to give a presentation in their city. If you get an invitation or if an announcement is made in your school, or some friend in another school tells you about the presentation, you do not have to be a student of that high school or buy their college counseling program to attend those presentations! If you are in doubt, email the college and ask if it is open to everyone. Boston University and NYU, for example, give presentations all over the world every year that are open to everyone who wants to learn more about BU and NYU. Don't miss this easy opportunity if you hear about any US college presenting in your city or country. It does not have to be on your "list;" just go and learn more about different colleges.

If you go: Take notes so that you can fill in your College Presentation Worksheets when you get home.

College Presentation Worksheets

Name of college 1: ______________________________

Date: ____________ Time: ____________

Location: ______________________________

Evaluated or information exchange? ______________________________

Name of presenter: ______________________________

Email: ______________________________

What is her/his responsibility (college admissions rep, alumnus, student, other): ____________

My impression of the college: ______________________________

Other questions I want to ask later by email: ______________________________

Thank-you note (by email): ______________________________

Date mailed: ______________________________

Name of college 2: ____

Date: ____________ Time: ____________

Location: ________________________________

Evaluated or information exchange? ________________

Name of presenter: ________________________

Email: ________________________________

What is her/his responsibility (college admissions rep, alumnus, student, other): ____________

My impression of the college: ____________________

Other questions I want to ask later by email: ______________________

Thank-you note (by email): ____________________

Date mailed: ____________________________

Name of college 3: ____

Date: ____________ Time: ____________

Location: ______________________________

Evaluated or information exchange? ________________

Name of presenter: ________________________

Email: ______________________________

What is her/his responsibility (college admissions rep, alumnus, student, other): ____________

My impression of the college: ____________________

Other questions I want to ask later by email: ______________________

Thank-you note (by email): ____________________

Date mailed: ____________________________

Name of college 4: ____

Date: ____________ Time: ____________

Location: ______________________________

Evaluated or information exchange? ________________

Name of presenter: ________________________

Email: ______________________________

What is her/his responsibility (college admissions rep, alumnus, student, other): ____________

My impression of the college: ____________________

Other questions I want to ask later by email: ______________________

Thank-you note (by email): ____________________

Date mailed: ___________________________

Name of college 5: ____________________

Date: __________ Time: __________

Location: ____________________

Evaluated or information exchange? ____________________

Name of presenter: ____________________

Email: ____________________

What is her/his responsibility (college admissions rep, alumnus, student, other): __________

My impression of the college: ____________________

Other questions I want to ask later by email: ____________________

Thank-you note (by email): ____________________

Date mailed: ____________________

Name of college 6: ______________________________

Date: ____________ Time: ____________

Location: ______________________________

Evaluated or information exchange? ____________________

Name of presenter: ______________________________

Email: ______________________________

What is her/his responsibility (college admissions rep, alumnus, student, other): ____________

My impression of the college: ____________________

Other questions I want to ask later by email: ______________________________

Thank-you note (by email): ____________________

Date mailed: ______________________________

College Campus Visits

Step 5: Search college campuses – think and fill in your College Visit Worksheets

Some of you will be lucky enough to visit a few college campuses in your search for your final college list. The first rule for you to remember is that you are spending the time and money to get there to do much more than to take photos back to your friends. You are there to learn with your own eyes and ears more about the campus and how you would feel being there. When is the best time to visit? For most students, the best time is when the students are there and going to class. But for students coming from a long distance, the best time is whenever you have the opportunity to visit a college. It may be during your winter holiday or in the summer. It may be junior year or early in senior year. It could be senior year before you have your final list or even in senior year after you have already applied. It will still be worthwhile because it will help you to decide where you are going to accept after you have heard from the colleges where you applied.

Don't even think of going on campus without finding out the time of the admissions information session for students and their families, the time of the student-led tours of the campus. If possible, ask to attend a class. When you are on a tour, be prepared with questions for the student guide. When you go to the dining hall, notice who is sitting with whom. Are the young women at one table and the young men at another? Are the athletes sitting together only with other athletes? Are students all mixed up racially? Are they in small and large groups? Are some students sitting alone, some in twosomes? Can you imagine where you will be sitting when you are there? Looking at a dormitory, are young men and women separated by buildings, by floor, by room? Do they share the same bathrooms? What would you prefer if you were there? When you get to the athletic facilities, notice who is in the fitness rooms. Ask if students can use the swimming pool any time of day? Are there recreational sports for beginners? Take a look at your Campus Visit Worksheet before you get on campus.

Online Campus Visit

If you cannot travel to the colleges before you apply, check out a video tour of college campuses. The video will add a visual look for your Final List. Many students and educators who live too far away for a visit, like these two Online Tours:

1. http://www.campustours.com
2. https://www.youniversitytv.com

Both are educationally sound and highly regarded resources for online college visits.

Campus Visit Worksheet

College 1: ______________________________

Address: ______________________________

Date of visit: ______________

Time of information session: ____________ Time of student tour: ____________

Questions For The Tour Guide

Name and email address of tour guide: ______________________________

What do you like best about your college? ______________________________

What do you wish you could change about your college? ______________________________

____

____

What's the food like? ______________________________

____

____

What do you do on the weekends? ______________________________

____

____

Where do you study? ______________________________

Where do international students go for Thanksgiving holiday? ______________

Are black and Asian students accepted in the sororities and fraternities? ______________

Do freshman live in freshman dorms or are students mixed by class? ______________

Do students get to talk with their professors outside of class? ______________

Ask the admissions rep if she/he can find you the name and email address of a student from your high school or city.

____

____

What do I think? ______________ Will I add it to my final list? ______________

Campus Visit Worksheet

College 2: ____

Address: ____

Date of visit: ______________

Time of information session: ____________ Time of student tour: ____________

Questions For The Tour Guide

Name and email address of tour guide: ______________________________

What do you like best about your college? ______________________________

What do you wish you could change about your college? ____________________

____

____

What's the food like? ____

____

____

What do you do on the weekends? ______________________________

____

____

Where do you study? ______________________________

Where do international students go for Thanksgiving holiday? ______________

Are black and Asian students accepted in the sororities and fraternities? ______________

Do freshman live in freshman dorms or are students mixed by class? ______________

Do students get to talk with their professors outside of class? ______________

Ask the admissions rep if she/he can find you the name and email address of a student from your high school or city.

____

____

What do I think? ____________________ Will I add it to my final list? ____________

Campus Visit Worksheet

College 3: ______________________________

Address: ______________________________

Date of visit: ______________

Time of information session: ____________ Time of student tour: ____________

Questions For The Tour Guide

Name and email address of tour guide: ______________________________

What do you like best about your college? ______________________________

What do you wish you could change about your college? ______________________________

____

____

What's the food like? ______________________________

____

____

What do you do on the weekends? ______________________________

____

____

Where do you study? ______________________________

Where do international students go for Thanksgiving holiday? ______________

Are black and Asian students accepted in the sororities and fraternities? ______________

Do freshman live in freshman dorms or are students mixed by class? ______________

Do students get to talk with their professors outside of class? ______________

Ask the admissions rep if she/he can find you the name and email address of a student from your high school or city.

____

____

What do I think? ______________ Will I add it to my final list? ______________

Final List of Ten Colleges

Step 6: Make your final list of 10 colleges.
By the end of junior year, you should have a good idea of your final list of ten to twelve colleges to which you are going to apply. Don't hurry to close the list. Take your junior year and September and October of your senior years to keep learning more about your choices. Fill in the questions from your research and in senior year; you will write your applications from this list.

College 1
1. What I like most: ____________________
2. What I don't like: ____________________
3. Favorite majors: ____________________
4. Special things I like about this college: ____________________
5. Percentage of international students: ____________________
6. Required TOEFL or IELTS: ____________________

College 2
1. What I like most: ____________________
2. What I don't like: ____________________
3. Favorite majors: ____________________
4. Special things I like about this college: ____________________
5. Percentage of international students: ____________________
6. Required TOEFL or IELTS: ____________________

College 3
1. What I like most: ____________________
2. What I don't like: ____________________
3. Favorite majors: ____________________
4. Special things I like about this college: ____________________
5. Percentage of international students: ____________________
6. Required TOEFL or IELTS: ____________________

College 4

1. What I like most: ______________________________
2. What I don't like: ______________________________
3. Favorite majors: ______________________________
4. Special things I like about this college: ______________________________
5. Percentage of international students: ______________________________
6. Required TOEFL or IELTS: ______________________________

College 5

1. What I like most: ______________________________
2. What I don't like: ______________________________
3. Favorite majors: ______________________________
4. Special things I like about this college: ______________________________
5. Percentage of international students: ______________________________
6. Required TOEFL or IELTS: ______________________________

College 6

1. What I like most: ______________________________
2. What I don't like: ______________________________
3. Favorite majors: ______________________________
4. Special things I like about this college: ______________________________
5. Percentage of international students: ______________________________
6. Required TOEFL or IELTS: ______________________________

College 7

1. What I like most: ______________________________
2. What I don't like: ______________________________
3. Favorite majors: ______________________________
4. Special things I like about this college: ______________________________
5. Percentage of international students: ______________________________
6. Required TOEFL or IELTS: ______________________________

College 8

1. What I like most: ______________________________

2. What I don't like: ______________________________

3. Favorite majors: ______________________________

4. Special things I like about this college: ______________________________

5. Percentage of international students: ______________________________

6. Required TOEFL or IELTS: ______________________________

College 9

1. What I like most: ______________________________

2. What I don't like: ______________________________

3. Favorite majors: ______________________________

4. Special things I like about this college: ______________________________

5. Percentage of international students: ______________________________

6. Required TOEFL or IELTS: ______________________________

College 10

1. What I like most: ______________________________

2. What I don't like: ______________________________

3. Favorite majors: ______________________________

4. Special things I like about this college: ______________________________

5. Percentage of international students: ______________________________

6. Required TOEFL or IELTS: ______________________________

Part III: Communications
Applications, Essays, and Interviews

Applications

You've got your final college list–10 to 12 colleges where you are going to apply. They are all places you know well enough to tell them apart by the time you complete each unique application. Your final list must give you different levels of selectivity so that you will be sure to have a couple of choices in April, when decisions are sent to you. No one knows the levels of selectivity that colleges accept better than your school counselor – your college counselor. No matter who else gives you advice, you will want to work closely with your school, guidance, or college advisor. (Whatever your high school calls the person responsible for college admissions.)

The dean has already read your high school transcript and test scores, and so you are in the group of "qualified" students who have the necessary academics to do the work at her/his college. Your application is the very first thing that the college reads from YOU. This is where you use everything that you've learned in "Part I: Self-Assessment" and "Part II: Searching the Colleges." You are going to think about who you are and where you want to go as you complete your applications. "Part III: Communications" gives you the chance to show how you are different from the hundreds of other applicants who are applying. This is where the college deans select from 6% to 60% of the students from the 85% who are qualified to do the work. Everyone knows the essay is important in this selection; everyone does not know how important the application is. Therefore, this book is going to help you be creative, think about who you are, what the college is like, and take your time to write out your fit with each of your 10 applications. And speaking of "write out," be sure to write out all of your exercises in complete sentences and good English. It is important for you to practice your self-assessment exercises, applications, and essay exercises in well-written sentences. You need the practice!

In "Part III, Communication Skills," take a look at the Application Organizer form. First of all, choose if you are going to use the Common Application, the Universal Application, the Coalition Application, or the School Application. The colleges say the application you choose makes no difference to them. I always tell students that if the college spends the time, creativity, and money on creating their own application, use it! If not, go with the Common. Keep track of each college application you complete with the Application Organizer. Write in the different test requirements, deadlines, recommendations to be sent, test scores to be sent. Use this book to keep accurate records so that all requirements are fulfilled by the deadline of the application.

Next you must decide if you are going to apply to one of the early plans or the regular plan. There are so many myths about the value of applying early that it's hard for you to believe what's best. No matter what you do, don't get stuck on, "I have to go early!" Even if you decide to apply early, try to think of 8 to 10 first choices. An early decision closes your mind. If you think 10 first choices, you will learn more about each college and write a stronger application for each of them. If you think 10 first choices, that means that you will always get into your first choice!

Before you start writing your application, think about what the deans of admission are looking for when they read applications. They already know you can do the work at their college by reading your transcript which was sent by your high school. Next, they want to know what special contribution you can bring to their campus life. The application asks you about your family, your school and community activities, your thoughts on your major and future career, your work experience, honors you've earned, and an opportunity to add something not requested. It also asks for school record, test scores, recommendations to be sent in at your request to your college office, and your essay. Sometimes a personal statement as well as an essay is requested. You will have some flexibility in filling in your thoughts on your major and career, summer and holiday experiences, and "other relevant information" not requested that you would like admissions to know about you.

Besides the essay, the application often includes questions asking for one paragraph or shorter answers. Most students slide over these, but here's another opportunity for you to get the edge and get in.

How can you be creative about your application? When it asks your intended major and career ideas, rather than check computer science or literature, check "Undecided." And when you have a space for Personal Statement or Personal information not yet requested, write a few words about your academic interests, such as, "I like math, foreign languages, or history best but not sure about my major. Or I am not sure what career it will lead me to." The point is that your college education will open your mind to many possibilities that you are unaware of as a high school student. Most Americans have no idea what their career will be. How could you? Who knows what the career opportunities are going to be five or ten years from now? Who knows what new careers you are going to think about after two years of college?

When asked about work experience, if you haven't worked for pay, use that space to explain any volunteer work that you did, or whatever you learned during your holidays from the experiences you had with family, friends, and or traveling.

When asked for "Anything else not requested that we should know," think of something that other students won't include; something specifically you, such as your interest in politics, working on an election, a bike trip, or your particular interest in art or literature or robot competitions. It could be reading, starting a club, or a family tradition or holiday that is important to you. These would be the unique things that only you can bring to the college culture. Uniqueness is what the college deans are looking for as they select one qualified student over another. Your job is to provide that difference on your application.

Take a look at the Common Application (p. 117) so that you can begin to think through different ways you can answer the questions that makes your application a creative one! Complete the form using a pencil so you can make changes. Use this form as a reference when you fill out your college applications.

Each college may have different deadlines for their application, test scores, teacher recommendations, and transcript. The Application Organizer you create will help you to keep track of each of your applications and keep it up to date until your applications are all in! You will be way ahead in your application process if you treat all college applications as a January application no matter if they are not due until February or March. Don't drag it out! Once you get the hang of it, keep going until all 8 or 10 applications with essay are completed and sent in.

Application Organizer

FINAL LIST (1)

School Name: ____________________

Your User Name: ____________________

Your Password: ____________________

School Codes

College Board: __________ ACT: __________

Admissions Rep for Your High School

Name: ____________________

Telephone: ____________________

Email: ____________________

Application Deadlines

Regular Decision: __________

Early Decision: __________

Restricted (Single Choice) Early Decision or Early Action: __________

Early Action: __________

Rolling Admissions: __________

Late Admissions (Waitlisted): May 1

Secondary School Report (SSR): __________

Teacher Recommendations Deadlines

Verbal Subject Teacher: __________

Math or Science Teacher: __________

Test Scores Sent

TOEFL or IELTS: __________

SAT or ACT: __________

SAT Subject Tests: __________

AP or IB Scores: __________

Interview Dates

____

____

FINAL LIST (2)

School Name: ______________________________

Your User Name: ______________________________

Your Password: ______________________________

School Codes

College Board: ____________ ACT: ____________

Admissions Rep for Your High School

Name: ______________________________

Telephone: ______________________________

Email: ______________________________

Application Deadlines

Regular Decision: ____________

Early Decision: ____________

Restricted (Single Choice) Early Decision or Early Action: ____________

Early Action: ____________

Rolling Admissions: ____________

Late Admissions (Waitlisted): May 1

Secondary School Report (SSR): ____________

Teacher Recommendations Deadlines

Verbal Subject Teacher: ____________

Math or Science Teacher: ____________

Test Scores Sent

TOEFL or IELTS: ____________

SAT or ACT: ____________

SAT Subject Tests: ____________

AP or IB Scores: ____________

Interview Dates

____

____

FINAL LIST (3)

School Name: ______________________________

Your User Name: ______________________________

Your Password: ______________________________

School Codes

College Board: ____________ ACT: ____________

Admissions Rep for Your High School

Name: ______________________________

Telephone: ______________________________

Email: ______________________________

Application Deadlines

Regular Decision: ____________

Early Decision: ____________

Restricted (Single Choice) Early Decision or Early Action: ____________

Early Action: ____________

Rolling Admissions: ____________

Late Admissions (Waitlisted): May 1

Secondary School Report (SSR): ____________

Teacher Recommendations Deadlines

Verbal Subject Teacher: ____________

Math or Science Teacher: ____________

Test Scores Sent

TOEFL or IELTS: ____________

SAT or ACT: ____________

SAT Subject Tests: ____________

AP or IB Scores: ____________

Interview Dates

____

____

FINAL LIST (4)

School Name: ______________________________

Your User Name: ______________________________

Your Password: ______________________________

School Codes

College Board: ______________ ACT: ______________

Admissions Rep for Your High School

Name: ______________________________

Telephone: ______________________________

Email: ______________________________

Application Deadlines

Regular Decision: ______________

Early Decision: ______________

Restricted (Single Choice) Early Decision or Early Action: ______________

Early Action: ______________

Rolling Admissions: ______________

Late Admissions (Waitlisted): May 1

Secondary School Report (SSR): ______________

Teacher Recommendations Deadlines

Verbal Subject Teacher: ______________

Math or Science Teacher: ______________

Test Scores Sent

TOEFL or IELTS: ______________

SAT or ACT: ______________

SAT Subject Tests: ______________

AP or IB Scores: ______________

Interview Dates

____

____

FINAL LIST (5)

School Name: ____________________

Your User Name: ____________________

Your Password: ____________________

School Codes

College Board: ____________ ACT: ____________

Admissions Rep for Your High School

Name: ____________________

Telephone: ____________________

Email: ____________________

Application Deadlines

Regular Decision: ____________

Early Decision: ____________

Restricted (Single Choice) Early Decision or Early Action: ____________

Early Action: ____________

Rolling Admissions: ____________

Late Admissions (Waitlisted): May 1

Secondary School Report (SSR): ____________

Teacher Recommendations Deadlines

Verbal Subject Teacher: ____________

Math or Science Teacher: ____________

Test Scores Sent

TOEFL or IELTS: ____________

SAT or ACT: ____________

SAT Subject Tests: ____________

AP or IB Scores: ____________

Interview Dates

____

____

FINAL LIST (6)

School Name: ______________________________

Your User Name: ______________________________

Your Password: ______________________________

School Codes

College Board: ________________ ACT: ________________

Admissions Rep for Your High School

Name: ______________________________

Telephone: ______________________________

Email: ______________________________

Application Deadlines

Regular Decision: ________________

Early Decision: ________________

Restricted (Single Choice) Early Decision or Early Action: ________________

Early Action: ________________

Rolling Admissions: ________________

Late Admissions (Waitlisted): May 1

Secondary School Report (SSR): ________________

Teacher Recommendations Deadlines

Verbal Subject Teacher: ________________

Math or Science Teacher: ________________

Test Scores Sent

TOEFL or IELTS: ________________

SAT or ACT: ________________

SAT Subject Tests: ________________

AP or IB Scores: ________________

Interview Dates

____

____

FINAL LIST (7)

School Name: ______________________________

Your User Name: ______________________________

Your Password: ______________________________

School Codes

College Board: ____________ ACT: ____________

Admissions Rep for Your High School

Name: ______________________________

Telephone: ______________________________

Email: ______________________________

Application Deadlines

Regular Decision: ____________

Early Decision: ____________

Restricted (Single Choice) Early Decision or Early Action: ____________

Early Action: ____________

Rolling Admissions: ____________

Late Admissions (Waitlisted): May 1

Secondary School Report (SSR): ____________

Teacher Recommendations Deadlines

Verbal Subject Teacher: ____________

Math or Science Teacher: ____________

Test Scores Sent

TOEFL or IELTS: ____________

SAT or ACT: ____________

SAT Subject Tests: ____________

AP or IB Scores: ____________

Interview Dates

____

____

FINAL LIST (8)

School Name: ______________________________

Your User Name: ______________________________

Your Password: ______________________________

School Codes

College Board: ______________ ACT: ______________

Admissions Rep for Your High School

Name: ______________________________

Telephone: ______________________________

Email: ______________________________

Application Deadlines

Regular Decision: ______________

Early Decision: ______________

Restricted (Single Choice) Early Decision or Early Action: ______________

Early Action: ______________

Rolling Admissions: ______________

Late Admissions (Waitlisted): May 1

Secondary School Report (SSR): ______________

Teacher Recommendations Deadlines

Verbal Subject Teacher: ______________

Math or Science Teacher: ______________

Test Scores Sent

TOEFL or IELTS: ______________

SAT or ACT: ______________

SAT Subject Tests: ______________

AP or IB Scores: ______________

Interview Dates

____

____

FINAL LIST (9)

School Name: ______________________________

Your User Name: ______________________________

Your Password: ______________________________

School Codes

College Board: ____________ ACT: ____________

Admissions Rep for Your High School

Name: ______________________________

Telephone: ______________________________

Email: ______________________________

Application Deadlines

Regular Decision: ____________

Early Decision: ____________

Restricted (Single Choice) Early Decision or Early Action: ____________

Early Action: ____________

Rolling Admissions: ____________

Late Admissions (Waitlisted): May 1

Secondary School Report (SSR): ____________

Teacher Recommendations Deadlines

Verbal Subject Teacher: ____________

Math or Science Teacher: ____________

Test Scores Sent

TOEFL or IELTS: ____________

SAT or ACT: ____________

SAT Subject Tests: ____________

AP or IB Scores: ____________

Interview Dates

____

____

FINAL LIST (10)

School Name: ______________________________

Your User Name: ______________________________

Your Password: ______________________________

School Codes

College Board: ____________________ ACT: ____________________

Admissions Rep for Your High School

Name: ______________________________

Telephone: ______________________________

Email: ______________________________

Application Deadlines

Regular Decision: ____________________

Early Decision: ____________________

Restricted (Single Choice) Early Decision or Early Action: ____________________

Early Action: ____________________

Rolling Admissions: ____________________

Late Admissions (Waitlisted): May 1

Secondary School Report (SSR): ____________________

Teacher Recommendations Deadlines

Verbal Subject Teacher: ____________________

Math or Science Teacher: ____________________

Test Scores Sent

TOEFL or IELTS: ____________________

SAT or ACT: ____________________

SAT Subject Tests: ____________________

AP or IB Scores: ____________________

Interview Dates

____

____

FIRST-YEAR APPLICATION

APPLICANT

Legal Name ______
Last/Family/Sur (Enter name **exactly** as it appears on official documents.) First/Given Middle (complete) Jr., etc.

Preferred name, if not first name (only one) ______ Former last name(s) ______

Birth Date ______ (mm/dd/yyyy) Sex ☐ Male ☐ Female

If you would like the opportunity, we invite you to share more about your gender identity ______

US Social Security Number, if any ______ E-mail Address ______
Required for US Citizens and Permanent Residents applying for financial aid via FAFSA

Preferred Telephone ☐ Home ☐ Mobile Home (____) ______ Mobile (____) ______
Area/Country/City Code Area/Country/City Code

Permanent home address ______
Number & Street Apartment #

______
City/Town County or Parish State/Province Country ZIP/Postal Code

If different from above, please give your current mailing address for all admission correspondence. (from ______ to ______)
(mm/dd/yyyy) (mm/dd/yyyy)

Current mailing address ______
Number & Street Apartment #

______
City/Town County or Parish State/Province Country ZIP/Postal Code

If your current mailing address is a boarding school, include name of school here: ______

FUTURE PLANS

Your answers to these questions will vary for different colleges. If the online system did not ask you to answer some of the questions you see in this section, this college chose not to ask that question of its applicants.

College ______

Entry Term: ☐ Fall (Jul-Dec) ☐ Spring (Jan-Jun) ☐ Other

Decision Plan ______

Academic Major & Interests ______

______

______

Career Interest ______

Deadline ______ (mm/dd/yyyy)

Do you intend to apply for need-based financial aid? ☐ Yes ☐ No

Do you intend to apply for merit-based scholarships? ☐ Yes ☐ No

Do you intend to be a full-time student? ☐ Yes ☐ No

Do you intend to enroll in a degree program your first year? ☐ Yes ☐ No

Do you intend to live in college housing? ______

What is the highest degree you intend to earn? ______

DEMOGRAPHICS

Citizenship Status: ☐ US Citizen or US National ☐ US Dual Citizen
☐ US Permanent Resident ☐ US Refugee or Asylee ☐ Other (Non-US)

Non-US Citizenship(s) ______

______

US Visa Status ______

Birthplace ______
City/Town State/Province Country

Years lived in the US? ______ Years lived outside the US? ______

Language Proficiency (Check all that apply.)
S(Speak) R(Read) W(Write) F(First Language) H(Spoken at Home)

	S	R	W	F	H
______	☐	☐	☐	☐	☐
______	☐	☐	☐	☐	☐
______	☐	☐	☐	☐	☐

Optional The items with a gray background are optional. No information you provide will be used in a discriminatory manner.

Religious Preference ______

US Armed Services veteran status & Dates of Service ______

______

1. Are you Hispanic/Latino?
☐ Yes, Hispanic or Latino (including Spain) ☐ No If yes, please describe your background.
______

2. Regardless of your answer to the prior question, please indicate how you identify yourself. (Check one or more and describe your background.)

☐ American Indian or Alaska Native (including all Original Peoples of the Americas)
Are you Enrolled? ☐ Yes ☐ No If yes, please enter Tribal Enrollment Number ______
______

☐ Asian (including Indian subcontinent and Philippines)
______

☐ Black or African American (including Africa and Caribbean)
______

☐ Native Hawaiian or Other Pacific Islander (Original Peoples)
______

☐ White (including Middle Eastern)
______

 AP-1

FAMILY

Please list both parents below, even if one or more is deceased or no longer has legal responsibilities toward you. Many colleges collect this information for demographic purposes even if you are an adult or an emancipated minor. If you are a minor with a legal guardian (an individual or government entity), then please list that information below as well. If you wish, you may list step-parents and/or other adults with whom you reside, or who otherwise care for you, in the Additional Information section.

Household

Parents' marital status (relative to each other): ☐ Never Married ☐ Married ☐ Civil Union/Domestic Partners ☐ Widowed ☐ Separated ☐ Divorced (date ________ yyyy)

With whom do you make your permanent home? ☐ Parent 1 ☐ Parent 2 ☐ Both ☐ Legal Guardian ☐ Ward of the Court/State ☐ Other

If you have children, how many? ________

Parent 1

☐ Mother ☐ Father ☐ I have limited information about this parent ☐ Other

Is Parent 1 living? ☐ Yes ☐ No (Date Deceased ________________ mm/yyyy)

____
Last/Family/Sur First/Given Middle

Former last name(s) ________________

Country of birth ________________

Home address **if different** from yours

____

____

Preferred Telephone: ☐ Home ☐ Mobile ☐ Work (______) ____________
Area/Country/City Code

E-mail ________________

Occupation (former occupation, if retired) ________________

____

College (if any) ________________ CEEB ________

Degree ________________ Year ________

Graduate School (if any) ________________ CEEB ________

Degree ________________ Year ________

Parent 2 *(optional)*

☐ Mother ☐ Father ☐ I have limited information about this parent ☐ Other

Is Parent 2 living? ☐ Yes ☐ No (Date Deceased ________________ mm/yyyy)

____
Last/Family/Sur First/Given Middle

Former last name(s) ________________

Country of birth ________________

Home address **if different** from yours

____

____

Preferred Telephone: ☐ Home ☐ Mobile ☐ Work (______) ____________
Area/Country/City Code

E-mail ________________

Occupation (former occupation, if retired) ________________

____

College (if any) ________________ CEEB ________

Degree ________________ Year ________

Graduate School (if any) ________________ CEEB ________

Degree ________________ Year ________

Legal Guardian *(if other than a parent)*

Relationship to you ________________

____
Last/Family/Sur First/Given Middle

Home address **if different** from yours

____

____

Preferred Telephone: ☐ Home ☐ Mobile ☐ Work (______) ____________
Area/Country/City Code

E-mail ________________

Occupation (former occupation, if retired) ________________

____

College (if any) ________________ CEEB ________

Degree ________________ Year ________

Graduate School (if any) ________________ CEEB ________

Degree ________________ Year ________

Siblings

Please give names and ages of your brothers or sisters. If they are enrolled in grades K-12 (or international equivalent), list their grade levels. If they have attended or are currently attending college, give the names of the undergraduate institution, degree earned, and approximate dates of attendance. If more than three siblings, please list them in the Additional Information section.

____
Name Age & Grade Relationship

College Attended ________________ CEEB ________

Degree earned or expected ________________ Dates ________________
mm/yyyy – mm/yyyy

____
Name Age & Grade Relationship

College Attended ________________ CEEB ________

Degree earned or expected ________________ Dates ________________
mm/yyyy – mm/yyyy

____
Name Age & Grade Relationship

College Attended ________________ CEEB ________

Degree earned or expected ________________ Dates ________________
mm/yyyy – mm/yyyy

AP-2

EDUCATION

Secondary Schools

Most recent secondary school attended ______________________________

Entry Date ____________ (mm/yyyy) Graduation Date ____________ (mm/yyyy) School Type: ☐ Public ☐ Charter ☐ Independent ☐ Religious ☐ Home School

Address ______________________________ (Number & Street) CEEB/ACT Code ____________

______________________________ City/Town State/Province Country ZIP/Postal Code

Counselor's Name ______________________________ Counselor's Title ____________

E-mail ____________ Telephone (______) ____________ ______ (Area/Country/City Code, Number, Ext.) Fax (______) ____________ (Area/Country/City Code, Number)

List all other secondary schools you have attended since 9th grade, including academic summer schools or enrichment programs hosted on a secondary school campus:

School Name & CEEB/ACT Code	Location (City, State/Province, ZIP/Postal Code, Country)	Dates Attended (mm/yyyy – mm/yyyy)

Please list any community program/organization that has provided free assistance with your application process: ______________________________

Please indicate if any of these options will have affected your progression through or since secondary school. Check all that apply and provide details in the Additional Information section. ☐ Did or will graduate early ☐ Did or will graduate late ☐ Did or will take time off ☐ Did or will take gap year

Colleges & Universities List all colleges/universities where you've taken courses since 9th grade and mark all that apply: taught on college campus (CO); taught on high school campus, excluding AP/IB (HS); taught online (ON); college credit awarded (CR); transcript available (TR); degree candidate (DC).

College/University Name & CEEB/ACT Code	Location (City, State/Province, ZIP/Postal Code, Country)	CO	HS	ON	CR	TR	DC	Dates Attended (mm/yyyy – mm/yyyy)	Degree Earned
		☐	☐	☐	☐	☐	☐		
		☐	☐	☐	☐	☐	☐		
		☐	☐	☐	☐	☐	☐		

If you indicated that a transcript is available, please have an official copy sent to your colleges as soon as possible.

ACADEMICS

The self-reported information in this **optional** section is not intended to take the place of your official records. Please note the requirements of each institution to which you are applying and arrange for official transcripts and score reports to be sent from your secondary school and the appropriate testing agencies. Where "Best Scores" are requested, please report the highest individual scores you have earned so far, even if those scores are from different test dates.

Grades Class Rank ________ (if available) Class Size ________ Weighted? ☐ Yes ☐ No GPA ________ (if available) Scale ________ Weighted? ☐ Yes ☐ No

ACT Exam Dates: (past & future) ________ mm/dd/yyyy ________ mm/dd/yyyy ________ mm/dd/yyyy
Best Scores: (so far) ________ COMP ________ mm/dd/yyyy ________ English ________ mm/dd/yyyy ________ Math ________ mm/dd/yyyy
________ Reading ________ mm/dd/yyyy ________ Science ________ mm/dd/yyyy ________ Writing ________ mm/dd/yyyy

SAT Exam Dates: (past & future) ________ mm/dd/yyyy ________ mm/dd/yyyy
Best Scores: (so far) ________ Critical Reading/ Evidence-based Reading and Writing ________ mm/dd/yyyy ________ Math ________ mm/dd/yyyy

TOEFL/ IELTS/PTE Exam Dates: (past & future) ________ mm/yyyy ________ mm/yyyy ________ mm/yyyy
Best Score: (so far) ________ Test ________ mm/yyyy ________ Score

AP/IB/SAT Subjects Best Scores: (per subject, so far)

mm/yyyy	Type & Subject	Score	mm/yyyy	Type & Subject	Score

Current Courses Please list all courses you are taking this year and indicate level (AP, IB, advanced, honors, etc.) and credit value. Indicate quarter classes taken in the same semester on the appropriate semester line. If you are not currently enrolled, please list courses from your most recent academic year.

Full Year/First Semester/First Trimester	Second Semester/Second Trimester	Third Trimester *or additional first/second term courses if more space is needed*

 AP-3

Honors *(optional)* Briefly list any academic distinctions or honors you have received since the 9th grade or international equivalent (e.g., National Merit, Cum Laude Society). S(School) S/R(State or Regional) N(National) I(International)

Grade level or post-graduate (PG) 9 10 11 12 PG	Honor	Highest Level of Recognition S S/R N I
☐☐☐☐☐		☐☐☐☐
☐☐☐☐☐		☐☐☐☐
☐☐☐☐☐		☐☐☐☐
☐☐☐☐☐		☐☐☐☐
☐☐☐☐☐		☐☐☐☐

EXTRACURRICULAR ACTIVITIES & WORK EXPERIENCE

Extracurricular *(optional)* Please list your **principal** extracurricular, volunteer, and work activities **in their order of importance to you**. Feel free to group your activities and paid work experience separately if you prefer. Use the space available to provide details of your activities and accomplishments (specific events, varsity letter, musical instrument, employer, etc.). **To allow us to focus on the highlights of your activities, please complete this section even if you plan to attach a résumé.**

Grade level or post-graduate (PG) 9 10 11 12 PG	Approximate time spent: Hours per week	Weeks per year	When did you participate in the activity? School year	Summer/ School Break	Positions held, honors won, letters earned, or employer	If applicable, do you plan to participate in college?
☐☐☐☐☐			☐	☐		☐
Activity						
☐☐☐☐☐			☐	☐		☐
Activity						
☐☐☐☐☐			☐	☐		☐
Activity						
☐☐☐☐☐			☐	☐		☐
Activity						
☐☐☐☐☐			☐	☐		☐
Activity						
☐☐☐☐☐			☐	☐		☐
Activity						
☐☐☐☐☐			☐	☐		☐
Activity						
☐☐☐☐☐			☐	☐		☐
Activity						
☐☐☐☐☐			☐	☐		☐
Activity						
☐☐☐☐☐			☐	☐		☐
Activity						

 AP-4

WRITING

Personal Essay

Note: Some colleges require a personal essay. You may submit a personal essay to any college, even if it is not required by that college.

Instructions. The essay demonstrates your ability to write clearly and concisely on a selected topic and helps you distinguish yourself in your own voice. *What do you want the readers of your application to know about you apart from courses, grades, and test scores?* Choose the option that best helps you answer that question and write an essay of no more than 650 words, using the prompt to inspire and structure your response. Remember: 650 words is your limit, not your goal. Use the full range if you need it, but don't feel obligated to do so.

- Some students have a background, identity, interest, or talent that is so meaningful they believe their application would be incomplete without it. If this sounds like you, then please share your story.
- The lessons we take from obstacles we encounter can be fundamental to later success. Recount a time when you faced a challenge, setback, or failure. How did it affect you, and what did you learn from the experience?
- Reflect on a time when you questioned or challenged a belief or idea. What prompted your thinking? What was the outcome?
- Describe a problem you've solved or a problem you'd like to solve. It can be an intellectual challenge, a research query, an ethical dilemma—anything that is of personal importance, no matter the scale. Explain its significance to you and what steps you took or could be taken to identify a solution.
- Discuss an accomplishment, event, or realization that sparked a period of personal growth and a new understanding of yourself or others.
- Describe a topic, idea, or concept you find so engaging that it makes you lose all track of time. Why does it captivate you? What or who do you turn to when you want to learn more?
- Share an essay on any topic of your choice. It can be one you've already written, one that responds to a different prompt, or one of your own design.

Additional Information *(optional)*

Please attach a separate sheet if you wish to provide details of circumstances or qualifications not reflected in the application.

Disciplinary History

Please Note: Common Application member colleges carefully consider all parts of your application. Information provided below will be considered in the context of the rest of your application and does not necessarily prevent you from being admitted to college. For more information on whether specific colleges choose to receive this information or how it may be considered, please contact the college directly.

① Have you ever been found responsible for a disciplinary violation at any educational institution you have attended from the 9th grade (or the international equivalent) forward, whether related to academic misconduct or behavioral misconduct, that resulted in a disciplinary action? These actions could include, but are not limited to: probation, suspension, removal, dismissal, or expulsion from the institution. ☐ Yes ☐ No

② Have you ever been adjudicated guilty or convicted of a misdemeanor or felony? ☐ Yes ☐ No
[Note that you are not required to answer "yes" to this question, or provide an explanation, if the criminal adjudication or conviction has been expunged, sealed, annulled, pardoned, destroyed, erased, impounded, or otherwise required by law or ordered by a court to be kept confidential.]

If you answered "yes" to either or both questions, please attach a separate sheet of paper that gives the approximate date of each incident, explains the circumstances, and reflects on what you learned from the experience.

Note: Applicants are expected to immediately notify the institutions to which they are applying should there be any changes to the information requested in this application, including disciplinary history.

SIGNATURE

Application Fee Payment If this college requires an application fee, how will you be paying it?

☐ Online Payment ☐ Will Mail Payment ☐ Fee Waiver Request

Required Signature

☐ *I certify that all information submitted in the admission process—including this application and any other supporting materials—is my own work, factually true, and honestly presented, and that these documents will become the property of the institution to which I am applying and will not be returned to me. I understand that I may be subject to a range of possible disciplinary actions, including admission revocation, expulsion, or revocation of course credit, grades, and degree should the information I have certified be false.*

☐ *I agree to notify the institutions to which I am applying immediately should there be any change to the information requested in this application, including disciplinary history.*

☐ *I understand that once my application has been submitted it may not be altered in any way; I will need to contact the institution directly if I wish to provide additional information.*

☐ *I acknowledge that I have reviewed the application instructions for the college receiving this application. I understand that all offers of admission are conditional, pending receipt of final transcripts showing work comparable in quality to that upon which the offer was based, as well as honorable dismissal from the school.*

☐ *I affirm that I will send an enrollment deposit (or equivalent) to only one institution; sending multiple deposits (or equivalent) may result in the withdrawal of my admission offers from all institutions. [Note: students may send an enrollment deposit (or equivalent) to a second institution where they have been admitted from the waitlist, provided that they inform the first institution that they will no longer be enrolling.]*

Signature ______________________________ Date ______________
mm/dd/yyyy

Common Application member institution admission offices do not discriminate on the basis of race, color, ethnicity, national origin, religion, creed, sex, age, marital status, parental status, physical disability, learning disability, political affiliation, veteran status, or sexual orientation.

College Essays

The purpose of a college admissions essay is to help admissions deans get to know you. The American college deans are looking to create a class of students who will fit their particular campus culture well–academically and socially. They are not looking to admit a class full of top testers and students who all think alike and don't mix with other students. Instead, the colleges want to find students who can add their point of view to the classroom discussion that will balance the other students' points of view and help strengthen their university. As a student from a particular family, high school, state, or country, you have experienced a unique education and homelife–your essay is a place to share some part of that experience. The colleges want to know: WHO IS THIS KID?

Whichever question you choose, make sure you are looking inward. What do you think? What do you value? What has made you grow as a person? What makes you the unique person the admissions deans will want to invite to join their campus community? The best essays spend significant time with self-assessment, and they don't spend a lot of time describing a place or event. Writing "What I have learned from the place or event" will reveal the thinking skills that describe a student's character, the character of a promising college student.

The good news is that you are not expected to sound like a genius with perfect test scores who has won the Nobel Prize in physics or literature in your spare time. You are not expected to come up with a vocabulary on the college essay that you would never use in conversation. Your assignment is much more simple. The essay should sound like you and reveal a real part of yourself. It should be well written. It does not need to be perfect. So, you need to think about what college admissions deans might enjoy learning about your story and start writing!

Write one essay at a time (350-500 words, typed, double-spaced). Wait a few days before you write another, and another few days before you write a third. The questions all require personal opinions. There are no right or wrong answers. The college is looking to learn more about you. They already know your academic record and test scores. Now they want to get to know how you think and what interests you. What is a student brought up in your home and school going to bring to their campus that is different from what your classmates who are also applying to the same college can bring? An essay exercise starts on the next page.

The admissions dean wants to know about you. It should be an essay that is a reflection of you, not the people and events in your life. In other words, if you write about your dad, or grandmother, or a bike trip that you took last summer—no matter how dramatic—tell about the person or event in a short paragraph and use the rest of the essay to tell what you learned from the person or experience. Explain how you've changed because of it. No matter what the question—who or what has influenced you the most—the task is not to write about the "who" or the "what." The college admissions dean wants to know what you learned from the "who" or the "what." Your college essay documents how you stand out from your friends and all those other seniors applying to Selective U!

Be yourself and go with the essay that has the most "you" in it. Trust yourself!

You Can Do This!

When you have written three essays, show your English, history, or social science teacher and get some feedback on your writing style. Not your ideas, but your writing style. Remember this: No matter the question, the colleges want to know your personal opinion. They want to know if you are an interesting person, a good student, and a hard worker, who will bring your own way of thinking to their particular college campus.

Essay Exercises

Essay 1: Why do you want to go to college?

THINK before writing: The college wants to know why you want to go to college. Ask some of your friends why they want to go to college. There are no right answers, because the college wants to know about YOU, and, ideally, your answer won't be the same answer as most of the other students. It's OK to say it's your natural next step, just as it was for your siblings and parents.

It is Tuesday afternoon at school and you are sitting in English class. Your teacher makes an announcement, "School will be closed tomorrow. The building will not be open. There will be no homework given and no tests when you return on Thursday." Hooray! You have a free day with no schoolwork to worry about.

Essay 2: How will you spend your day?

THINK before writing: The college wants to know your interests and activities outside of school. Writing how you spend your free time tells a lot about your interests and what you value. Remember that the activity is not the most important part of this essay, but what you learn from the activity is. You will want to write why you would spend your day doing what you want to do, and what you will learn from it (relaxation and fun counts, too!).

Essay 3: Write about an incident or time when you made a mistake or experienced failure. How did it affect you, and what lessons did you learn?

THINK before writing: This question may seem to go against everything that you have learned at home and school. It is much easier to tell about successes and winning than it is to think about mistakes and failure. For a mark of maturity, it is important to show your ability to learn from your mistakes. Be sure to spend the most time on your response to your mistake or failure and on how you learned and grew from the experience.

Essay 4: Describe a place or environment where you are most happy. What do you do or experience there, and why is it meaningful to you?

THINK before writing. A "place or environment" could be many things–a house, tree top, classroom, basketball court, family, country, stage, imagined space, book, or even an internal place in your head and heart. Think about where and when you are most happy, and then analyze the source of that happiness. Keep in mind that the "why" at the end of the question is essential. This essay, like all of the other essays, is asking you to look inward and share with the admissions deans what you value.

Essay Question 5: Why do you want to come to this college?

THINK before writing. Wait to write this essay when you have an idea of some of the colleges where you plan to apply. Name the college you are writing about. Many of your applications will have this question. The question is asking you what you know about their particular college. They want to know why you think it would be a good fit. Ranking, major, geography, and weather will not be good reasons. You have to know more than that about a college to write a winning application.

College Interview

Most students will have an interview online rather than on-campus. The colleges do not expect students to drive more than three hours to come to the college campus for an interview. Interviews are usually scheduled by the college after the student has sent in his or her application. Very few of you will have an interview on campus although some of you will have an interview with a graduate of the college or a college rep closer to where you live. Do not worry if you do not have an interview! For those of you who do have an interview on campus, in your city, or online, no matter who is interviewing for what college, they are all looking for the same thing. WHO IS THIS KID and how well does she or he communicate who they are? Here are some interview tips to keep in mind:

The Spoken Word

Interviews and getting together in person at a college fair, college presentation, or online with a college admissions representative (rep) are all part of the spoken–word component.

Do Interviews Count?

The interview policies vary so much that you will have to ask the college admissions dean: a. Do you require an interview? b. Where can I get an interview? c. Is the interview evaluated? If you have an interview, don't dread it. Think conversation–this is not a grilling session or a search for right answers. Do not memorize what you are going to say! Whatever you say in the interview must make sense to you. If you aren't comfortable with a question asked, say something that you are comfortable about. In any kind of interview, your goal is always the same: a. to make sense and b. to show high interest in the particular college.

Have some hard facts at hand about the academics and any of your special interests in music, theater, sports, or publications. Have some personal questions to ask the college rep that aren't easily answered on their website. Showing strong interest is an important factor in being accepted by selective colleges.

How do I prepare for questions I may be asked? The best preparation for your interview is to look back to the self-assessment exercises and read over your answers. Be prepared to talk about your strengths and traits that need improvement, as well as your interests and special talents. Next, look at the particular statistics of the college that you researched. If you are going to interview for a college that is not on your list be sure to go back and research it before you go to the interview. Review everything you wrote in the "College Search Section II." Be prepared to ask the interviewer questions about the college. Bring a list of your questions with you for your interview. Here are some that you may want to ask, in addition to any special interest questions that you are concerned about:

Examples of questions for you to ask the college interviewer:

1. What do students like most about your college?
2. How many sophomores and juniors live on campus?
3. When will I get a roommate?
4. What are the most popular majors on campus? The smallest majors?
5. How do most students spend their time on weekends?
6. How are roommates matched?
7. Do you have theme housing options for freshman?
8. How do freshman register?
9. Do you have faculty advisors for class registration?
10. What is most special about your college?
11. What do students like best about the college?
12. Are there health care services on campus?

Remember that interviews are a two-way exchange. Try to think of the interview as a conversation rather than a question-and-right-answers session. Here are tips straight from what the college reps complain about!

- Turn off your cell phone before you go into the interview!
- Don't even think of looking at your phone during the interview.
- Don't chew gum.
- Watch your language. Try to use the best grammar that you know, but don't worry about using words that you don't ordinarily use in conversation. Remember that the interviewer doesn't look for vocabulary words you studied for testing.
- Your parents will be more interested in what you wear than the college will. You don't need to "dress up" for a college interview. Keep in mind that a good impression always helps. Clean, casual school clothes will work well, not torn or ripped jeans. Arrive on time, shake hands firmly, sit and stand straight, and act confident and happy to be there. Even if you are worried, try not to show it, ask the interviewer questions until you are more relaxed.

Admissions interviews are your opportunity to sell yourself. Make a friend of the interviewer. Look him in the eye. Be straightforward and relaxed in your conversation. Don't try to say "what you think they want to hear." Be confident that there are no "right" answers or directions for the interview. They want to know you better. Your attitude toward learning is what they want to know most. Also:

- Do you have a sense of humor?
- Do you have the ability to overcome tough situations?
- What do you know about their college?
- Are you the kind of student who can take advantage of the educational opportunities at this selective college?
- How high is your interest in attending the college? What kind of match will you make in their college community?
- How will you manage your time and life when you get away from home and on your own?
- How will you spend your out-of-class time?

Have clear goals that you are able to discuss honestly. Some common questions they may ask: What interests you about our college? What are you looking for in a college? What are your educational goals? Why should we accept you? What do you expect to contribute to our college community?

<u>Do not</u> give excuses for poor grades or explain how you're going to do better next semester. Lead from your strengths. For example, talk about your love for reading, sports, a beautiful campus, classics, politics, your pride in your family, your achievements, your dog-training techniques, your summer school experience, your sports awards, your favorite newspaper, your favorite section of the newspaper, and/or the business you started.

Take time to listen to the questions, and answer them directly. It's hard, but try not to worry about silence. Collect your thoughts. Tell the admissions person that you are eager to go to college and what you like about this college.

Go to the interview with your goal clearly in your mind: to distinguish yourself and to be sure that the dean of admissions is clear that you are interested in getting into this college." Trust yourself–your personal thoughts and opinions and your own voice. You are the one that the college wants to get to know. If you are comfortable with the conversations that you have with the interviewer, you can be sure that you did well.

Interview Exercises

Online Interview:

Name of college: ______________________________

Date and time: ____________________

Who is interviewing me (admissions officer, alumnus, student)? ____________________

Evaluated or information exchange? ____________________

Name of interviewer: ______________________________

Email address: ______________________________

My impression of the college: ______________________________

____

____

Other questions I want to ask later by email: ____________________

____

____

Thank-you email: ______________________________ Date mailed: ____________

On-/Off-Campus Interviews

Name of college: ______________________________

Date and time: ____________________ Location: ____________________

Evaluated or information exchange? ____________________

Name of interviewer: ______________________________

Telephone number: ______________________________

Email address: ______________________________

Who is interviewing me (admissions officer, student)? ____________________

My impression of the college: ______________________________

____

____

Other questions I want to ask later by email: ____________________

____

____

Thank-you email: ______________________________ Date mailed: ____________

Online Interview:

Name of college: ____________________

Date and time: ____________________

Who is interviewing me (admissions officer, alumnus, student)? ____________________

Evaluated or information exchange? ____________________

Name of interviewer: ____________________

Email address: ____________________

My impression of the college: ____________________

____

____

Other questions I want to ask later by email: ____________________

____

____

Thank-you email: ____________________ Date mailed: ____________________

On-/Off-Campus Interviews

Name of college: ____________________

Date and time: ____________________ Location: ____________________

Evaluated or information exchange? ____________________

Name of interviewer: ____________________

Telephone number: ____________________

Email address: ____________________

Who is interviewing me (admissions officer, student)? ____________________

My impression of the college: ____________________

____

____

Other questions I want to ask later by email: ____________________

____

____

Thank-you email: ____________________ Date mailed: ____________________

Online Interview:

Name of college: ______________________________

Date and time: ______________________________

Who is interviewing me (admissions officer, alumnus, student)? ______________________________

Evaluated or information exchange? ______________________________

Name of interviewer: ______________________________

Email address: ______________________________

My impression of the college: ______________________________

____

____

Other questions I want to ask later by email: ______________________________

____

____

Thank-you email: ______________________________ Date mailed: ______________

On-/Off-Campus Interviews

Name of college: ______________________________

Date and time: ______________________________ Location: ______________________________

Evaluated or information exchange? ______________________________

Name of interviewer: ______________________________

Telephone number: ______________________________

Email address: ______________________________

Who is interviewing me (admissions officer, student)? ______________________________

My impression of the college: ______________________________

____

____

Other questions I want to ask later by email: ______________________________

____

____

Thank-you email: ______________________________ Date mailed: ______________

Online Interview:

Name of college: ____________________

Date and time: ____________________

Who is interviewing me (admissions officer, alumnus, student)? ____________________

Evaluated or information exchange? ____________________

Name of interviewer: ____________________

Email address: ____________________

My impression of the college: ____________________

____

____

Other questions I want to ask later by email: ____________________

____

____

Thank-you email: ____________________ Date mailed: ____________________

On-/Off-Campus Interviews

Name of college: ____________________

Date and time: ____________________ Location: ____________________

Evaluated or information exchange? ____________________

Name of interviewer: ____________________

Telephone number: ____________________

Email address: ____________________

Who is interviewing me (admissions officer, student)? ____________________

My impression of the college: ____________________

____

____

Other questions I want to ask later by email: ____________________

____

____

Thank-you email: ____________________ Date mailed: ____________________

Online Interview:

Name of college: ____________________

Date and time: ____________________

Who is interviewing me (admissions officer, alumnus, student)? ____________________

Evaluated or information exchange? ____________________

Name of interviewer: ____________________

Email address: ____________________

My impression of the college: ____________________

____

____

Other questions I want to ask later by email: ____________________

____

____

Thank-you email: ____________________ Date mailed: ____________________

On-/Off-Campus Interviews

Name of college: ____________________

Date and time: ____________________ Location: ____________________

Evaluated or information exchange? ____________________

Name of interviewer: ____________________

Telephone number: ____________________

Email address: ____________________

Who is interviewing me (admissions officer, student)? ____________________

My impression of the college: ____________________

____

____

Other questions I want to ask later by email: ____________________

____

____

Thank-you email: ____________________ Date mailed: ____________________

Online Interview:

Name of college: ______________________________

Date and time: ______________________________

Who is interviewing me (admissions officer, alumnus, student)? ______________________________

Evaluated or information exchange? ______________________________

Name of interviewer: ______________________________

Email address: ______________________________

My impression of the college: ______________________________

____

____

Other questions I want to ask later by email: ______________________________

____

____

Thank-you email: ______________________________ Date mailed: ______________

On-/Off-Campus Interviews

Name of college: ______________________________

Date and time: ______________________________ Location: ______________________________

Evaluated or information exchange? ______________________________

Name of interviewer: ______________________________

Telephone number: ______________________________

Email address: ______________________________

Who is interviewing me (admissions officer, student)? ______________________________

My impression of the college: ______________________________

____

____

Other questions I want to ask later by email: ______________________________

____

____

Thank-you email: ______________________________ Date mailed: ______________

Part IV
College Admissions Calendar

Juniors

SEPTEMBER

- Junior-year grades are the last finals completed for your transcript sent to colleges.
- Think about your special talents outside of school.
- Remember this: You are worth more than your test scores.
- International students: Check dates for TOEFL or IELTS tests.
- Check on dates for SAT or ACT and plan to take them in the spring.
- Check on college fairs coming to your school or city.
- Make a friend of your college counselor.

OCTOBER

- Attend college fairs and college presentations whenever possible.
- Buy one college guide describing US colleges from your local bookstore or online from www.barnesandnoble.com or www.amazonbooks.com.
  The Fiske Guide or *The Ultimate Best Colleges in America*
- Buy one college admissions process guide: *8 First Choices, third edition*, by Joyce Slayton Mitchell, author of *Who is this Kid?*

NOVEMBER

- If you haven't yet taken the SAT or ACT, register for one of the exams to take in the spring.
- International students, if you haven't yet taken the TOEFL or the IELTS, register to take it, as soon as possible.
- Study *The Fiske Guide* or *The Ultimate Best Colleges in America* and start "Search the Colleges" exercises for any three colleges.
- Attend a college fair or college presentation if available.

DECEMBER

- Continue researching college guides and read about new colleges.
- Write more self-assessment exercises in this book and fill in the "Search the Colleges" exercises.
- USE YOUR VACATION to continue researching the colleges that interest you.
- Take some time off from studying to do something new and interesting in your life.

JANUARY

- If you have not yet taken your TOEFL or IELTS exams, register and take them as soon as possible.
- If you have not yet taken your SATs or ACTS, register for this spring.
- Continue working on the exercises in this book.
- Keep up your best study habits, arts, athletics, jobs, and friendships.

FEBRUARY

- If you are in advanced or honors classes, and strong in a foreign language or art history and not taking an AP in those subjects, ask your teachers about taking the SAT Subject test in May. You do not have to be in an AP course to take the SAT Subject tests. Students who do exceptionally well in mathematics, a foreign language, or take a course outside of school can take any AP test without the class in high school. Check it out!
- Work on the exercises in this book.

MARCH

- Check your "Search the Colleges" exercises and start narrowing your list of 20.
- Check out the websites of the colleges that interest you most.
- Take an online tour of at least 12 colleges in the next three months.
- Check with students from other schools to find U.S. college fairs and presentations to attend.

APRIL

- Plan your courses for next year, include a foreign language, math, and science course if possible.
- Take more online college tours.
- Read and start writing the exercises for "Part I: Self-Assessment" in this book.

MAY

- Check out summer jobs, volunteer work, or travel. Remember this: EVERYTHING COUNTS on the college application. Everything. That includes mowing lawns, baby-sitting, home chores, milking cows, dog training and any other ways you spend your time. You will be writing about what you learned from the activity, not judged on what the activity is.
- Work on activities in this book.
- Finalize your college list to 10 or 12 colleges.
- Look for summer college fairs and presentations.

SUMMER MONTHS–JUNE, JULY, AUGUST

- Write application exercises specifically for each of your final list colleges. Give each college your special attention and equal time.
- Write essay exercises especially for each of your final list colleges. Give each college equal time, noticing the differences of each college.
- Notice and note all of your new and usual out-of-school activities.
- Check out school fairs and college presentations in your area to attend before school starts.
- Check out the websites of the colleges on your Final List.

Seniors

SEPTEMBER

- Fill in your Application Organizer in your Workbook, in "Part III: Communications." Write in all of the categories for your final ten colleges to which you are going to apply. Be sure you know enough about each college before you write an application. Consider each of those ten colleges as your first choice college as you write the application. You must be prepared to go to each of those colleges, because you do not know which choices you will have.
- If you are going to take one more test such as TOEFL or SAT or ACT, sign up now!
- Ask two teachers (one math/science, and one verbal) if they will write a college recommendation for each of your applications. Tell your teachers that they can use the same letter for each of your colleges. The recommendation letter should be sent in with your high school transcript by your college counselor. Students should NOT send the letter; most of you will not see the letter.
- Keep up your school work, remember this: first term of senior grades are the only senior grades the college reps see before their decisions to admit or reject.
- Send an email to your school's college rep of each of the colleges on your final list to ask if they are coming to your high school or nearby this fall. If they are, ask them when and where, and write that you and your parents would like to attend.

OCTOBER

- If you are applying for an Early Decision, Early Action, or Restricted Early Action plan, write those applications now. Check your Application Organizer for dates of all your colleges. Discuss earlies with your college counselor. NOTICE the agreement that you sign with an early application. You must follow the agreement that you made with your signature. The honesty and honor of your name always goes with a signature at the time that you sign.
- If some colleges on your list follow a Rolling Admission schedule, treat those as Early and write and send their application as well as the Early Plan application, only if permitted by the Early college to add "rolling or state colleges."
- Check your essays that you wrote during the summer; ask a teacher to look over your essay now.
- Check to see if any colleges are visiting your city and ask your friends in other high schools if any colleges are giving presentations in their schools.
- Attend any college fairs or presentations traveling near you if you are planning to apply.

NOVEMBER

- Recheck that your test scores are sent by The College Board or ACT to all of the colleges where you are applying.
- Give your teachers the college forms and verify that they know when and where to send them, check those recs out with your school counselor.
- Ask your guidance or college office to send your transcript by the date requested by the college. Each college can be different! So, it's your responsibility to know what is required when. Write it all in your Application Organizer in your book.
- Keep up your grades and friendships.

DECEMBER

- December 15th is the decision date for all Early programs. If you were accepted by your Early Decision choice, that's it! No more applications are allowed to go out. If you were accepted by your Early Action choice, you can decide now to apply no more or apply to one or two that you think you would like better. If you were deferred or denied early, send in the rest of your applications before your winter break. No matter what the deadline, treat all February or late January deadlines as if they are due by January 15th. Getting those applications in is important, so that you are free to focus on keeping up your grades.

JANUARY

- All of your applications should be mailed in January.
- If you have earned any awards or honors, be sure that information gets to each of your colleges where you applied.

FEBRUARY

- Check with your school counselor to be sure that you have done everything necessary to complete the application process.
- If you plan to take any AP exams in May, register now for a March deadline.

MARCH

- Most college decisions arrive toward the end of March. Be sure you wait until you know ALL of your schools' decisions before you make a move–you do not have to decide and deposit until May 1. While you are waiting–you will hear most of the decisions by the 10th of April–check out your Workbook and review what you know about each of your accepted colleges.
- This is the toughest month–the final waiting month to hear your college decisions. The more exercise, sports, biking, running, swimming you can find time for, the better you will be able to deal with the stress of waiting. It's especially hard because everybody keeps asking, "Where did you get in? Where are you going?" Just keep saying, "I haven't heard all of my decisions yet."

APRIL

- Ahhhhh! April! The power to choose is all yours. Now you know your choices. Some colleges will be nearby and all will offer presentations for their accepted students in April. A few of you will take a trip to the colleges to see them for the first time. Maybe you can go to two accepted programs. If so, go to two or three colleges that sound best to you. If you have an opportunity–go!
- Once you decide where you are going to go, mail your deposit check in to reach the college by May 1. Notify your other choices that you will not be attending so that other students will be invited to attend.
- If you are waitlisted for a college that you like as well or better than the one you accepted, then stay on the waitlist. Send a letter along with the card you are returning. In the letter say anything new that you have learned about why that college is your best fit, and send it along with the card that you must return to be on the waitlist. If you get accepted from the waitlist, you do not have to go to that college; you can remain at the college where you sent your deposit. Either way, you must notify the college that you will not be attending.
- Honesty is the best policy with deposits and waitlists. You have agreed that you will send only one deposit. You will want the colleges to know that your word, your agreement, your name is an honorable one–so follow the rules.

MAY

- Take your AP exams if you are registered for them.
- If you are on a waitlist, keep the college informed of your continuing interest.
- If you weren't accepted anywhere, see your school counselor and also go online and find colleges that are still accepting students. Many universities that you did not know about, that are fully accredited and have strong students attending them, will still have openings. Check them out!

JUNE

- Check with your college or guidance office and be sure your final transcript is sent to the college where you are attending.
- CONGRATULATIONS!!
- It's graduation time.

Part V
Glossary

College Admissions Talk–What Does it Mean? College Admissions has its own language. Here are some terms you should know.

Advanced Placement (AP): College-level courses offered in some high schools for which students may earn college credit. Students can qualify for advanced standing when they enroll in college; students may take the AP Exams in May whether they have taken the course or not.

American College Test (ACT): A college entrance test administered by the American College Testing Corporation. US colleges allow students to submit scores from either the ACT or SAT.

Arts and sciences (the liberal arts): This is the college within a university, or a separate college course of study, that includes the humanities, social sciences, natural sciences, mathematics, foreign languages, and fine arts. It's America's typical undergraduate college.

Candidates' reply date: The May 1 deadline, observed by the selective colleges by which the applicant must respond to one offer of admission with a deposit.

College Board: Administers the TOEFL, PSAT, the SAT, the SAT Subject Tests, and the Advanced Placement (AP) tests. The SATs are developed in arrangement with the Educational Testing Service (ETS).

Common Application, Universal Application, and Coalition Application: The Common Application form is accepted by more than seven hundred fifty colleges, often supplemented by the college's own form. It is available online at www.commonapp.org. The Universal Application, available online at www.universalcollegeapp.com/ is accepted by about fifty colleges. The Coalition Application is available online at www.coalitionforcollegeaccess.org. A major difference with this application is that students can begin the process of college admissions in ninth grade. About 175 colleges use the Coalition.

Consortium: A group of colleges and universities that offer joint programs, cross-registration for academic course work, and coordinated social, cultural, and athletic programs to the students within the affiliated group. For example: Amherst, the University of Massachusetts, Mount Holyoke, and Smith are the Four College Consortium.

Co-op job: An on-the-job training program, usually related to the student's major. Often a full-time, paid job with a semester or year off campus. Internships have replaced many of the co-op jobs in past years.

Core curriculum: A specified program of courses that all students must take to graduate.

Deferral: Postponement of applicants for early decision or early action that will be considered within the regular applicant pool. It is also a postponement for some students from the waitlist to defer until the next January, February, or even for a year.

Distribution requirements: Required courses for college graduation. Usually a student can choose from many courses within the categories of the humanities, social sciences, sciences, fine arts, foreign languages, and mathematics.

Early Action (EA): A program whereby students receive an early admission, deferral, or denial decision in December, but are not obligated to enroll if admitted. Boston College, Chicago, Georgetown, Harvard, MIT, Notre Dame, Princeton, Stanford, and Yale are best known for "single-choice" or "restricted early action "(REA).

Early Decision (ED): A program whereby students apply by the first or middle of November and receive an early admission, deferral, or denial decision in December and are obligated to enroll if admitted and if financial aid award is sufficient. If admitted, ED students are required to withdraw all other college applications. Increasingly colleges are offering a second or "late" early decision, with decisions given in February; some even offer a "late-late" ED.

ETS: Education Testing Service, Princeton, NJ; develops college entrance tests for the College Board.

Four-one-four: An academic calendar consisting of two regular four-month semesters with a short winter or January term in between.

Graduate student: A college student who has completed the bachelor's (BA, BS) degree and is working toward a master's (M.A., M.S.) or doctoral degree (M.D., Ph.D, JD).

Greek system: Fraternities and sororities on campus. They are called "Greek" because their names originate from letters in the Greek alphabet.

Humanities: Courses in which the primary focus is on human culture; this includes philosophy, foreign language, religion, and literature.

Interdisciplinary major: Combined majors such as political science, philosophy, and economics, or Spanish and business administration, often created and negotiated by students.

International Baccalaureate (IB): A precisely prescribed high school program originated in Geneva, Switzerland, which is available around the world. Students can earn advanced standing in American colleges.

Internships: An on-the-job training program, often related to the student's major. Usually a summer or weekend work opportunity. Sometimes a full-time, paid job with a semester or year off campus.

Language requirement: A foreign language graduation requirement at many colleges. Some colleges offer an option to place out of the requirement through examinations during freshman orientation week.

Legacy: An applicant whose parents or grandparents are graduates of a particular college. Siblings, uncles, and aunts are not usually considered legacy. Many colleges give academically qualified legacies an edge in admissions.

Liberal arts college: The college within a university or a separate college course of study that includes the humanities, social sciences, natural sciences, mathematics, foreign languages, and fine arts. It's America's typical undergraduate college.

Open admissions: A policy whereby any student with a high school diploma is accepted, usually a policy of public universities for resident students.

Pass-fail: An option to replace grades at some colleges to encourage students to take courses outside their major interests, and talents, and an option at some colleges for first semester of freshman year.

Quad: An abbreviation of "quadrangle" found on many traditional campuses, where the classroom or dorm complexes are built on a square or rectangle with a green in the center.

Quarter system: An academic calendar of four quarters (rather than the traditional two semesters), of which three constitute a full academic year; sometimes called the Dartmouth Plan, where students must attend one summer in the four years. This system encourages students to be more creative in their off-campus time, which can come any time of year, not only in the summer.

Resident Advisor (RA): A paid student personnel officer or an upperclassman living in a freshman dorm to offer support and advice to new students.

Residential college: A living unit within a larger institution that offers special academic programs to its students; best models are Rice and Yale. In public universities, a residential college is also called a living/learning community.

Restricted Early Action (REA): See Early Action.

Rolling admissions: An admissions policy by which a college evaluates and decides upon applicants as soon as the application is complete. Colleges often promise a decision within six weeks. Public universities are often rolling, although they can hold decisions until April for out-of-state students, and the dates tend to vary each year.

SAT and SAT Subject Test: Widely used college entrance examinations administered by the College Board and created by Educational Testing Service (ETS). The SAT: Reasoning Test measures critical reading and math logic. The SAT Subject Tests are one-hour tests measuring achievement in a particular course of study.

Score Choice: An option whereby students can choose which SAT and SAT Subject Test scores they want to send to the colleges.

Semester system: Two blocks of several months each, constituting a full academic year at most American colleges. Students take summers off.

Social sciences: College courses that deal with human society, including anthropology, economics, history, political science, psychology, and sociology.

Teaching Assistant (TA): A graduate student who teaches undergraduates, and/or holds smaller discussion sections or study groups in conjunction with a professor's lectures.

Three-two program (3-2): A program in which students study three years in a liberal arts college followed by two years at a specialized school. Examples are engineering, nursing, or business administration.

Trimesters: The academic calendar divided into three equal terms to constitute a full year.

Undergraduate: A college student working toward a bachelor's degree; usually a four-year program.

Waitlist: The list of students who are qualified to attend but not yet accepted. Many students get into the college they most want to attend from the waitlist.

Yield: The percentage of the accepted students who enrolled at a particular college. Some say that admissions are driven by yield, because colleges are often rated by how many students enroll from the accepted list.

Endorsements for Joyce Slayton Mitchell

Harvard: "Mitchell offers many great insights into the complexity of the college admissions process and what should be the overriding concerns of the vital issue of the match between the student and the college."
–William R. Fitzsimmons, Dean of Admissions

Connecticut College: "Joyce Slayton Mitchell has won my heart with this thoughtful and practical guide to the college admissions process. Her advice is straight up and free of gimmicks—a rarity found in today's college admissions resource books."
–Martha C. Merrill, Dean of Admission and Financial Aid

Northwestern: "Trust Joyce Slayton Mitchell. Her advice gives everyone—students, their parents, and their counselors—the 'can do' confidence to get through college admissions without meltdown. Read this book in sections and read some of it out loud. You'll like what you hear. Ms. Mitchell knows the hearts—and minds—of students and their parents."
–Sheppard Shanley, Senior Associate Director of Admissions

Lynn University: "It's a how-to-with heart—less about gimmicks and more about caring for the student and his or her experience of the admissions process. The approach is quite sane and really very helpful."
–Delsie Z. Pillips, VP for Enrollment

Carleton: "Mitchell provides a strong personal advocacy for student decision making in the college-search process. If you can compare the search for the right college in 21st-century America to a wild, white water rafting ride, then you want this author as your river guide. There are . . . uncertainties, unseen rocks, and too many rapids among the many options facing young people in choosing a just-right college. Ms. Mitchell places the decision-making process squarely in the hands of . . . student[s] and provides the most useful tips for guiding their choice process. It is well done and [a] must read for every college-bound student."
–Paul Thiboutot, Dean of Admissions

Smith: "Eight First Choices" makes a scientist out of the high school senior who sets out to collect data until she finds her eight perfect matches. America's vast college resources are highlighted as this book shows students how to measure all of our different campus cultures."
–Audrey Y. Smith, Director of Admission

University of Michigan: "This is one of the finest publications about college admissions that has come out in some time. The author was able to apply her extensive knowledge of the real issues that create anxiety among students and parents and artfully provide an effective road map to help students navigate their way though the college admission process."
–Ted Spencer, Director of Admissions

Macalester: "Mitchell offers a primer on how to help the deans get to know you. She convincingly makes the point that the key to ending up with a satisfying final college choice relies on the student's approach to the process—critical self-examination, thorough research, complete investigation, plenty of organization, and an open mind throughout."
–Lorne T. Robinson, Dean of Admissions

Duke: "For many years Joyce Slayton Mitchell has given outstanding advice to families seeking guidance through the college admissions maze. And we in the admissions profession have enjoyed her valuable insights, sharp opinions, and clear writing as she has examined the college selection process. This thoughtful and well-organized book, which distills her years of experience, is no exception."
–Christoph Guttentag, Dean of Admissions

Dickinson College: "After thirty years in college admissions, including at Colgate and Johns Hopkins, I know that highly selective college admissions has become superficial—colleges are now arrogant ('maybe you just might be good enough to get in, maybe not') and the students are myopic ('I must get into an Ivy university or I will be nothing'). And in my thirty years, I have read countless books claiming an insider's view and advice. Way too much clutter for profit, and too short on sound advice that is student centered. Enter Joyce Slayton Mitchell and Eight First Choices. This is a must read for the very bright student who thinks 'Prestigious U' is the only place for her, as well as the above average student who is scared to death that he won't be accepted anywhere. Mitchell tells it like it is—it's about the students's learning style and educational objectives, and about discovering the range of college options to find the right fit. I speak often and around the country on the same topics. Nobody does it better than Mitchell."
–Robert J. Massa, Vice President for Enrollment

Haverford: "Joyce Slaton Mitchell is very knowledgeable about the constant changes in the admission profession. Her overall expertise and emphasis on student ownership of the admission process is invaluable for anyone applying to selective colleges and universities."
–Michael J. Keaton, Senior Associate Director of Admission

University of Pennsylvania: "This is the only book that puts you, as the college applicant, at the center of the admissions process. Eight First Choices will encourage you to be philosophical, thoughtful, and strategic about your college choices."
–Eric J. Kaplan, former Director of Admissions

Rice: "The most interesting and practical guide I have read in many years. A 'must read' for students and parents entering the college admission process."
–Richard N. Stabell, former Dean of Admission

Indiana University: "What a terrific resource for students and families! Eight First Choices is such a comprehensive, balanced, step-by-step guide to the college selection process, with an emphasis on the research and self-assessment necessary for assuring a good match. Use the extensive expertise and personal knowledge of Joyce Slayton Mitchell as you begin and complete your college search!"
–Mary Ellen Anderson, Director of Admissions

Standford: "Joyce Slayton Mitchell is a real teacher. She uses the college selection process as a learning experience for students. She tells her students up front that they are going to learn a great deal about themselves and what's important to them. As a result, they have a much better college selection experience. For students and parents undertaking the college application process, I can think of no better guide. This book distills [Mitchell's] wisdom into 208 pages, and provides a most valuable piece of sanity and wisdom."
–Robin Mamlet, former Dean of Admission

University of Pittsburgh: "Eight First Choices offers wise advice about the college search process culled from decades of counseling experience by Joyce Slayton Mitchell. This stress-busting book infuses the reader with hope and energy on the first premise, 'you are in charge,' provides practical advice on how to make this happen, and ends with the affirmation, 'be authentically and specifically you.' Mitchell's indeed right, selecting the right college can and should be an adventure in self-learning and she provides a step-by-step practical guide to getting the job done right. Give yourself a gift – make full use of this expert's advice."
–Betsy Porter

Emory: "During my twenty-one years at Emory, I have benefited greatly from Joyce Slayton Mitchell's wise, accurate, and compassionate view of college admissions. Listen to what she says; she gets it right and she knows what's most important in all of this: the students!"
–Scott L. Allen, Associate Dean, Director of International Recruitment

Colgate: "There are those who have been trying to sell their publications by trying to lead college-bound applicants and their families into believing that making the best college selection is as simple as reading a list or two of ill-conceived rankings. For the applicant who is serious about doing meaningful research and reading valuable suggestions about how to indentify colleges and universities that could be ideal matches, Joyce Slayton Mitchell's excellent book is exactly what they should be reading. The bottom line, though, is that Eight First Choices is a terrific piece of work."
–Gary L. Ross, Dean of Admissions

Wesleyan: "This book brings the advice of one of the great college counselors to many who need it most—and haven't typically had the advantage. You could read the first five pages and be a leg-up in the process. But don't stop there! JSM knows what she is talking about, writes clearly in an easy-to-follow format, and shares very good, practical information that will help every student be successful in making the next step to college. I have given many copies to friends and family to help pave the way for a successful college search."
–Nancy Hargrave Meislahn, former Dean of Admission and Financial Aid